Praise for C

"Far too many men are compromising their purity and forfeiting their God-given power to finish well. Why? The enemy is vehemently attacking God's original plan for our sexuality. In this book, my friend Dr. Doug Weiss expertly exposes the enemy's tactics and arms you to fight back. Men, it's time to take a stand. It's time to come clean."

— John Bevere, author
and speaker, Messenger
International

"As I see it, the substance of this book provides four things: (1) a forthright, God-fashioned Sword-of-Truth that will bring freedom to men who seek sexual fulfillment without compromising sexual purity; (2) a handbook for continuing wholeness of mind, soul, and body that will build husbands who love their wives, honor their families, and are successful in their workplaces; (3) a pastoral resource for revival in a local church as the lead pastor lives and leads the men of his flock toward living out its content and growing unto the fruitful life it will unfold; and (4) the seeds of potentially recoverable single and married people who are mired in the muck of a society drenched with sexual confusion, corruption and condemnation. There are revivals in this book; renewal for individuals, congregations, communities and—may God grant it—a nation!"

— Jack W. Hayford, founder
and chancellor, The King's
University–Los Angeles

"In our church we have been ministering to men caught in sexual addiction for over ten years. What I like about Doug, and what I love about *Clean* is that it isn't just more theory. It's filled with practical, usable tools for men who desire to live in victory and sexual integrity! Read it. Practice it. You will find the help you need."

— James M. Reeves, DMin, senior pastor, City on a Hill (Formerly Celebration Fellowship), Ft. Worth, Texas; author of *Refuge*

"*Clean* is going to change anyone outside or inside the Church struggling with sexual addictions. This book is a breath of fresh air as it gives practical tools to help men and woman overcome the sexual addiction epidemic from a biblical perspective. You will understand what sexual addiction is and how to overcome it. *Clean* will give you hope when you thought you had none. My testimony is evidence that these principles you are holding really work."

— Cory M. Schortzman, LPC, SRT, president, speaker, author, therapist, Transformed Hearts Counseling Center, Inc.

"Dr. Doug Weiss has done it again. Gathering from his own story and the account of others, he has parlayed his counseling experience into an exceptional tool to help you walk clean. As a pastor, husband, and father, I know firsthand the necessity for victory in this area, without which the American church will become ineffective in bringing healing to the home."

— Glenn Shaffer, senior pastor, DestinyLifeChurch.tv

"*Clean* is a much needed addition to the men's ministry arsenal. This book outlines in simple, easy to understand, and usable terms strategies for men to live the overcoming Christian life."

— Neville A. Brooks,
senior pastor, Jubilee
International Ministries,
Pittsburgh, Pennsylvania

"I have seen men's lives and families be transformed throughout the Kansas City area by using the tools and principles outlined in this book. I believe every Christian household could benefit by utilizing the book as a guide for their families as they navigate through our sexualized culture."

— Steve Fugate, founder
of Freedom KC

"Dr. Doug Weiss has walked the walk, talked the talk, and is beckoning our nation to stand up with him in victory and come 'clean.' This resource offers men, marriages, families, and churches, the hope, encouragement, practical tools, and 'how to' necessary to be victorious after they have been devastated, silenced, torn apart, and destroyed as a result of breaches in sexual integrity. I highly recommend *Clean* as a timely, empowering resource for men, spouses, pastors, and leaders, with proven biblical strategies for sexual integrity."

— Linda Wilkinson, associate
pastor—Pastoral Care,
Kelowna Christian Center

"Sexual sin can be overcome. Doug Weiss shows us biblical teachings that guide us to a new life as we walk with God. I have seen the results using his work, now let us go do HIS work."

— Rev. James McGinnis,
the Tabernacle, Orchard
Park, New York

"No one has walked the walk for over 25 years and is able to talk the talk as well as Doug Weiss. His insight and deep revelations are the reward for his commitments and a treasure of wisdom for each of us desiring to be clean."

— Nathan McClintock,
Life Central Church,
Plano, Texas

"As a pastor and marriage counselor I have seen the devastation that sexual compromise and addiction can cause for men, women, families, and churches. There is not a more qualified individual than Dr. Doug Weiss to equip believers and churches to overcome this insidious evil. This book is a fantastic resource that I hope every believer reads and every church uses to address this issue."

— Jimmy Evans, founder
and CEO, MarriageToday

"Doug Weiss speaks biblical, commonsense truth to the hearts of men and helps us to see all women through the eyes of God rather than our own selfish eyes. I know so many men who have wrestled for years with how to become clean in the area of their sexuality, and Doug has developed a vital resource to help men discover the freedom that is theirs because of the grace of God. It's time to stop hiding and start to get clean!"

— Kirk Giles, president,
Promise Keepers Canada

"Over many decades millions of people have struggled and continuously lose the battle for their sexual integrity. Many who have been celebrated as public successes have ended up on the floor defeated as private failures. As a result many families and reputations have been tragically destroyed. Over the last 25 years, my friend Doug Weiss (a former victim himself) has fought and won the battle for sexual purity. In this book *Clean*, he shares time-tested and proven strategies of how to reclaim our lives, families, and churches back from the enemy's stronghold."

— Dr. Sola Fola-Alade,
pastor, Trinity Chapel,
London, United Kingdom,
and CEO of www
.empowermentuniversity.com

Clean

Clean

A PROVEN
PLAN *for* **MEN**
COMMITTED TO
SEXUAL INTEGRITY

Doug Weiss, PhD

THOMAS NELSON
Since 1798

NASHVILLE   DALLAS   MEXICO CITY   RIO DE JANEIRO

Published in Nashville, Tennessee, by Thomas Nelson. Thomas Nelson is a registered trademark of Thomas Nelson, Inc.

Author is represented by the literary agency of Alive Communications, Inc., 7680 Goddard Street, Suite 200, Colorado Springs, CO 80920, www.alivecommunications.com.

Thomas Nelson, Inc., titles may be purchased in bulk for educational, business, fund-raising, or sales promotional use. For information, please e-mail SpecialMarkets@ThomasNelson.com.

Unless otherwise noted, Scripture quotations are taken from the Holy Bible, New International Version®, NIV®. Copyright © 1973, 1978, 1984 by Biblica, Inc.™ Used by permission of Zondervan. All rights reserved worldwide. www.zondervan.com

Scripture quotations marked MSG are from *The Message* by Eugene H. Peterson. © 1993, 1994, 1995, 1996, 2000. Used by permission of NavPress Publishing Group. All rights reserved.

Scripture quotations marked KJV are from the King James Version (public domain).

Scripture quotations marked RSV are from the REVISED STANDARD VERSION of the Bible. © 1946, 1952, 1971, 1973 by the Division of Christian Education of the National Council of the Churches of Christ in the U.S.A. Used by permission.

Library of Congress Cataloging-in-Publication Data

Weiss, Douglas.
  Clean : a proven plan for men committed to sexual integrity / Doug Weiss.
     p. cm.
  Includes bibliographical references (p.   ).
  ISBN 978-1-4002-0468-7
1. Husbands—Sexual behavior. 2. Sex addiction—Religious aspects—
Christianity. 3. Sex—Religious aspects—Christianity. 4. Husbands—Religious
life. I. Title.
  BV4528.3.W45 2013
  241'.6640811—dc23   2012038969

Printed in the United States of America

HB 01.26.2024

This book is dedicated to my brothers
and their clean destinies.

Joshua, standing before the angel, was dressed in dirty clothes. The angel spoke to his attendants, "Get him out of those filthy clothes," and then said to Joshua, "Look, I've stripped you of your sin and dressed you up in clean clothes."

—Zechariah 3:3–4 MSG

Contents

Introduction

My Life as an Addiction Counselor

In more than twenty years of counseling, I have found one thing to be true: life can be hard. I know, because I see "difficult" walk through my door every day. I see men who have allowed their lives to spiral out of control, and as they hit rock bottom, they become desperate for help. I also see brokenhearted women, shocked at what they have just learned about the men they married. Blindsided by a secret sexual betrayal, these ladies then wonder how they will survive. Their husbands' lives now mirror the bird in the ancient proverb that flies into a snare, "little knowing it will cost him his life" (Proverbs 7:23).

I also know there is a way out. I have seen it. It's a way of life that will restore the honesty, integrity, and strength that these husbands and wives both crave. We all enjoy the feeling of being clean, free, living with a clear conscience and no secrets.

The apostle Peter alluded to this kind of freedom that comes with repentance when he spoke to the crowds in the book of Acts, "Repent, then, and turn to God, so that your sins may be wiped out, that *times of refreshing* may come from the Lord" (Acts 3:19, emphasis added).

But this type of internal transformation requires work. More work than most people are used to. Nevertheless, if both the husband and wife stay the course and do the work, slowly over time they *will* see results. Trust can be rebuilt. I see it all the time.

I also see a lot of church leaders struggling to help those trapped in the cycle of sexual sinning, whether it's porn or adultery or something else. But many church leaders fall to sexual temptation themselves, and the ones who do stay pure are often at a loss as to how to help those struggling. As a result, I travel and speak at many of these churches, encouraging the leadership to confront the issue head-on because, whether they know it or not, it *is* embedded somewhere in their church. The rooting-out process can be painful, but if a community of believers is willing to go the extra mile for one another, get real, and extend grace, they will soon see the blessing of the Lord return to their sanctuary. You see, with

God there are no secrets. He already knows—everything. That's why I am excited about the message of this book. It's what I like to call "the road map to redemption," a tried-and-true system that will create a culture of honesty and integrity in churches and families.

So let me ask you, do you have the courage to become clean? Do you want to see your wife smile again? Would you like to be able to look others in the eye? Would you like to regain trust with your family and community? Then read the following pages with intense focus and resolve to do the necessary work.

Maybe you're single. Great. If you have never been married and you picked up this book, then you're ahead of the game. There are plenty of life lessons and instructions for you in *Clean*. If you are willing to conquer your fears and begin to live a life of sexual integrity, you, too, will experience the blessing of God. And you will provide your future spouse with a priceless gift—a wholly devoted, transparent, clean companion.

Perhaps you are recently divorced and wondering if you will ever find love again. *Clean* will also help you. The book of Joel says, "I will repay you for the years the locusts have eaten" (2:25).

That can be true of your life, if you are willing to own your past and believe in the possibility of a new future.

To the men who are already clean, I need you to read

these pages for your brothers in the body of Christ. An epidemic of sexual sickness has invaded every local church. In these pages you will find many helpful paradigms and biblical teachings that will help you help your brothers.

You will find the Lord giving you insights in how to communicate ideas that help men get and stay clean. You can be an important warrior in the fight for sexual purity in the church. So read, take notes, share with your brothers, and become instrumental in winning this war.

No matter who you are, it all comes down to doing the work. Tom Landry, a famous professional football coach for the Dallas Cowboys, knew this truism. During his tenure, his teams made it to multiple playoff and championship games. While he made everything look easy on the outside, always maintaining a calm demeanor, he had a saying about leading his players: "Leadership is getting someone to do what they don't want to do, to achieve what they want to achieve."[1] He knew his players had to show up at practice and do the work if they wanted to win. The same is true with getting clean. It's hard work, but the end result is well worth it. Unfortunately, most people find it easier to stay hidden in a sinful lifestyle than to be honest with themselves.

For those of you willing to embark on this journey, I applaud you. It takes great courage for you to first admit there is a problem and then to commit to doing something about it. You won't regret it. God will honor your hard work.

After all, isn't that what Jesus did for us? He chose to face the difficulty of the cross so that we could be with him forever. He laid down his life. Will you now lay down your life for him?

I think he's worth it.

A Dirty War Declared

Legend has it that there was a day not so long ago when men were more sexually pure. There was a day when a man gave his word on his wedding day to forsake all others, and he did exactly what he said he would do. He stayed married and faithful to the wife God gave to him to cherish. In that day, it was expected that men would keep their word to their wives and to others. A man was as good as his word, as the stories say.

There was a day when a man would run from wicked women and avoid the porn store located on the dirty side of town. Some with grey hair still talk of the era when a man's word was as good as gold. Then the war started. This wasn't a conventional war with bombs, planes, and navy ships, raised by some faraway nation. This war was raised against us, the church and our culture, from the very pit of hell itself.

The enemy of our souls began a sexual campaign—or as we would later call it, a sexual revolution. This campaign would question the very core biblical view of sexuality. The vicious weapons of pornography, drugs, and sexual immorality were raised against our educational institutions and churches, and the onslaught spread throughout the land. The fight pitted sons and daughters against the truths and values of their parents and grandparents like no other cultural war in the history of mankind. These young people talked of free love, or rather free sex. Pornography was a right and sex was a right without consequences or responsibilities.

This mind-set developed in many ways over the next decades. The Internet has taken this sexual combat to every home, computer, and cell phone. For most of us men, pornography is only a click away, and it grants the enemy's army easy access to our hearts, lives, and families.

This has an impact on every church in this great nation and many nations around the world. Some churches are active in the fight against sexual sin, and some have no idea they are in a war; half or more of their men are dead inside because their silent sins are keeping them from reaching their full destiny in Christ.

Clean is a solution manual for all of you engaged in this great war. You didn't ask for it; you just happened to be born when the enemy declared murderous intentions on you and your family, church, and nation. You had no say, but you are called to help our God set free a generation. No church community in history has had to reckon with such an intense and sophisticated inundation of sexual perversity. And we are God's only warriors in this battle. Our culture says we are crazy to believe God's Word about sexual fidelity and purity, whether we are single or married.

If we win this war together, we might see a return to Christian sexual values in our culture. We might return to a day when sexual purity is the standard once again, and perversion is seen for the damaging entity it really is. After I share with you some sobering statistics about our precarious situation, I will take you through this warrior's manual to help you get and stay free your entire life, and to help your brothers in Christ.

I write this handbook from a place of absolute compassion. I never met my father. I was placed in foster homes, sexually abused, and fully sexually addicted as a teen and young adult. I know the damages of this enemy personally. This soldier has the scars and has experienced the shame of feeling flawed and disconnected from God and the body of Christ, much like many of you do. The memories of this war are real for me, and so is the victory I will share with you in future pages. Victory is so much sweeter, since this is what God has made each of us for—*victory*!

I have been sexually clean for more than twenty-five years. I have not masturbated, viewed pornography, or had any sexual behavior outside of my marriage. My clean lifestyle has been validated repeatedly by a polygraph, so I am telling you the truth man to man, soldier to soldier.

You may ask, "Why a polygraph?" Well, several years ago when my pastor fell sexually, one of the female group leaders in my office began to wonder who she could trust. After all, her husband was unfaithful and her pastor as well as mine was also unfaithful. She sincerely asked me if I was really clean. I wanted everyone to know the other clinicians in my office as well as myself are clean. So all of the counselors agreed to take a polygraph annually to verify our years of sexual freedom. We felt that this was the least we could do for those hurt by this pastor's falling.

In the last two decades of counseling men who were sexually addicted, their wives, and families who were impacted by the man's addiction, I have seen the ravages of this war. You could fill a room with the tears I have witnessed from the men, women, and children who have been wounded. I have also seen the miracle of men getting clean and staying clean and their marriages and families healed, and I have written several books related to sexual addiction. I am considered an expert in the field of recovery, having appeared on *Oprah*, *Dr. Phil*, and many other national television shows, and I've even had a Lifetime Network movie made about our treatment for sex addicts called *Sex, Lies and Obsession*. I am also the president of the American Association for Sex Addiction Therapy (AASAT). We train and certify counselors and life coaches to help those who struggle with sexual addiction both nationally and internationally.

The book you're holding contains tested and tried weapons for you to get and stay clean, not for a week, month, or year, but for the rest of your life. Our culture needs men committed to win this war, today more than ever, and my prayer is that you would answer that call, for those you love and who trust you to be a man of God.

I am now going to take you through an introduction to relevant facts and statistics, and then in the following chapters give you the tools to be that sexually clean man you deserve to be. Even if you never struggled in this area, please read and join the men who need help to see them cross over the finish line and hear "well done, good and faithful servant," by our precious Lord and master Jesus Christ (Matthew 25:23).

Statistics

Many of us older guys grew up in a totally different world than the one we have today. In those days, you were likely to never see porn in your adolescence, unless you had an adult neighbor or family member who left it around. Today pornography is available on every cell phone connected to the Internet and on computers everywhere, and that doesn't even include the magazines on full view at convenience stores.

So, how big is this monster we are talking about? One comprehensive online article, "Internet Pornography Statistics," compiled by Jerry Ropelato, has much to say about this. Unless otherwise noted, the facts in this section are attributed to this resource.[1] It's a great way to get a broad overview of this subject.

Pornography Time Statistics

- Every second, $3,075.64 is being spent on pornography.
- Every second, 28,258 Internet users are viewing pornography.
- Every second, 372 Internet users are typing adult search terms into search engines.
- Every 39 minutes, a new pornographic video is being created in the United States.

I don't know about you, but I think three thousand dollars a second is a lot of money. In one hour, that would add up to $10,800,000. Given those statistics, you don't have to be a mathematician to understand porn brings in an enormous income per year. Sadly, some of this money is coming right out of the wallets of churchgoers. Let's look at the money being spent on a national scale.

2006 Worldwide Pornography Revenues	
Country	Revenue (Billions)
China	$27.40
South Korea	$25.73
Japan	$19.98
US	$13.33

2006 Pornography United States Industry Revenue Statistics (in Billions)	
Video Sales & Rentals	$3.62
Internet	$2.84
Cable/PPV/In-Room/ Mobile/Phone Sex	$2.00
Exotic Dance Clubs	$2.19
Novelties	$1.73
Magazines	$0.95
Total	$13.33

Now that we have seen some of the financial aspects of pornography, let's walk through frequency and scope of

Internet searches on sex and porn, as well as get a broader look at the sexual side of the Internet.

2006 Top Adult Search Requests		
Search Term	2006 Search Requests	Web Pages Containing Keywords (Millions)
Sex	75,608,612	414.00

Demographics		
Search Term	Male	Female
Sex	50%	50%
Porn	96%	4%

Internet Pornography Statistics	
Pornographic websites	4.2 million (12% of total websites)
Pornographic pages	420 million
Daily pornographic search engine requests	68 million (25% of total search engine requests)
Daily pornographic e-mails	2.5 billion (8% of total e-mails)

Internet users who view porn	42.7%
Received unwanted exposure to sexual material	34%
Average daily pornographic e-mails/ user	4.5 per Internet user
Monthly pornographic downloads (peer-to-peer)	1.5 billion (35% of all downloads)
Youths who received sexual solicitation	1 in 7 (down from 2003 statistic of 1 in 3)
Worldwide visitors to pornographic web-sites	72 million visitors

America leads the way as the top producer of video and DVD pornography. Also, we are number one in porn Web pages. In 2006, the United States had 244,661,900 porn Web pages. The next largest producer of porn pages is Germany, with ten million porn Web pages. This dubious type of world leadership on pornography has come to pass during many of our lifetimes. This tragedy signals a shift in history. I am sure you agree leading the world on this matter is not the leadership you and I desire for our nation or for our children. The question is, what will we do with this battle? Will we fight it, be taken captive by it, or simply ignore this attack on God's bride, the church?

Men and Pornograpy

Now let's take a short look at some realities about men and pornography viewing. The Internet Filter Learning Center (2008) states "It is estimated that approximately 13% of the US population regularly views Internet pornography, 75% of whom are males."[2]

Christian men also have issues with looking at pornography. A speaker at one Christian conference noted: "At a recent men's conference in Southern California, nine out of ten of the 565 men in attendance said that lust, pornography, and fantasizing were the habitual, continual, or fatal disconnecting factor in their relationship with God."[3]

These statistics are alarming. If 90 percent of the men at a Christian conference see this as a big issue in their relationship with God, we all need to take this war seriously. If we do not mobilize those of us who believe porn hurts, no one will grow. Even worse, Christian men could easily grow coldhearted and believe that viewing pornography is not even a sin. The Word of God has several admonitions about lusting after women as sin, and yet pornography is corrupting even this most basic Christian belief.

Women

Men today are not the only ones viewing pornography. In the last decade, my office treated more female sex addicts than in the previous decade.

Women and Pornography	
Women keeping their cyber activities secret	70%
Women struggling with pornography addiction	17%
Ratio of women to men favoring chat rooms	2X
Percentage of visitors to adult websites who are women	1 in 3 visitors
Women accessing adult websites each month	9.4 million
Women admitting to accessing pornography at work	13%

Clergy

The next category of porn viewers is pastors. Half of the pastors or their wives at churches where I have been a member have fallen to sexual sin during my thirty years as a Christian. This reflects our current reality; but thankfully many pastors, priests, and clergy do not struggle in this area.

This is evident in statistics collected by Dr. Lynn Anne Joiner in her work, "Congregants' Responses to Clergy Pornography Addiction":

> Surveys of Protestant evangelical clergy in the United States reported that 33% to 43% admitted to viewing Internet pornography (Gardner, 2001; Reed 2001). Of these numbers, approximately 6% to 18% viewed pornography multiple times per month and one survey cited 37% of clergy who described Internet pornography as a current temptation (Reed, 2001).[4]

The National Coalition for the Protection of Children and Families reports,

> In an informal survey of pastors in Seattle, Washington, conducted by the National Coalition for the Protection of Children and Families (2000), 11 percent of the 58 pastors surveyed intentionally had accessed a sexually explicit website; 9 percent viewed by choice and felt that it may be a problem for them. Five thousand pastors were questioned through the website www .pastors.com, and 55 percent indicated that they had

visited a pornographic site within the last year; 33 percent had visited a sexually explicit site within the previous three weeks.[5]

According to national surveys by *Christianity Today* and *Leadership Journal,* porn viewing is an issue for some clergy today.

In a nationwide survey conducted by *Christianity Today,* 4 in 10 pastors with Internet access reported they have visited a pornographic Web site . . . and more than one-third have done so in the past year. Slightly over half of the pastors (51%) say Internet pornography is a temptation for them; 37% admit it is a current struggle. Among the laity, 11% report at least occasionally viewing pornography.[6]

I love pastors. While I was in seminary working on my master's in divinity degree, I was also an associate pastor. I have nothing but compassion for pastors who struggle with pornography or sexual issues. Over the past twenty-five years, I have worked with many pastors who have gotten and stayed clean. I have seen their churches grow amazingly after they were free in this area of their lives. One counselor in my office has a telephone therapy group just for pastors, and he is so proud of those who walk out their purity alongside their brothers and colleagues.

I also have great respect for pastors who have taken some heat for talking about these issues or starting groups in their churches for men who struggle. Pastors are a major part of the solution to helping the bride of Christ become clean without stain. My hat is off to all of them. If you have a pastor, encourage him or her in the ministry of the local church.

Young People

A study done in 2009 by Deborah Braun-Courville and Mary Rojas states that in the United States, the percentage of young people looking at sexually explicit material ranges from 56 percent to 86 percent of young men and 31 percent to 56 percent of young women. But apparently, "rates of pornography use among females are increasing, with nearly half of female adolescents reporting viewing pornography in the past 6 months."[7]

Viewing of pornography has ramifications. Young people today have been impacted significantly by viewing pornography.

Pornography can affect each adolescent differently. In years of counseling I have seen many men significantly attach to early images. This subject of the impact on adolescents was also a discussion in the US Senate. The US Senate Subcommittee on the Constitution, Civil Rights and Property welcomed Jill C. Manning's testimony on the impact of pornography on family life in 2005. She offered this disturbing information:

> When a child or adolescent is directly exposed to pornography the following effects have been documented:
>
> 1. Lasting negative or traumatic emotional responses.
> 2. Earlier onset of first sexual intercourse, thereby increasing the risk of STDs over the lifespan.
> 3. The belief that superior sexual satisfaction is attainable without having affection for one's partner, thereby reinforcing the commoditization of sex and the objectification of humans.
> 4. The belief that being married or having a family are unattractive prospects.
> 5. Increased risk for developing sexual compulsions and addictive behavior.
> 6. Increased risk of exposure to incorrect information about human sexuality long before a minor is able to contextualize this information in ways an adult brain could.
> 7. And overestimating the prevalence of less common practices (e.g. group sex, bestiality, or sadomasochistic activity).[8]

In 2008 the National Campaign to Prevent Teen and Unplanned Pregnancy teamed up with the website

Cosmogirl.com to present a study on "Sex and Tech," which offers these statistics:[9]

- 20% of teens overall have sent or posted videos or pictures of themselves that are either nude or seminude.
- 39% of teens post or send messages that are sexually suggestive.
- 71% of teen girls and 67% of teen guys say they have either posted or sent content that is sexually suggestive to a boyfriend/girlfriend.
- 21% of teen girls and 30% of teen boys have sent sexual content to a potential boyfriend/girlfriend.
- 15% of teens have sent or posted nude/seminude images of themselves to someone they never met.
- 51% of teen girls as compared to 15% of teen boys say pressure from the opposite sex is a reason they send sexual messages or images.
- 23% of teen girls and 24% of teen boys say friends pressured them to post or send sexual content.
- 66% of teen girls and 60% of teen boys cite the most common reason for sending sexually suggestive content is to be "fun or flirtatious."
- 40% of teen girls say it was "a joke" to send sexually suggestive content, messages or images.
- 34% of teen girls say they "feel sexy" when they post/send sexually suggestive content.

- 38% of teen girls and 39% of teen boys say they have had sexually suggestive e-mails or texts shared with them that were originally meant for someone else
- 25% of teen girls say they have had images that were nude or seminude shared with them that were originally meant for someone else.

All the statistics we have covered are shocking, but especially those about our young people. They are the future of our church and our society. If this trend continues, the majority of young people will be scarred by the most diverse and perverse pornography in world history. Now is the time to become and stay clean, and to give hope to our sons and daughters so they can shine the light of Christ to their generation.

Children Internet Pornography Statistics	
Average age of first Internet exposure to pornography	11 years old
15–17 years old: having multiple hard-core exposures	80%
8–16 years old: have viewed porn online	90% (most while doing homework)

Wow. I know it's a different world from the way many of us grew up. However, this is the real world, and the future generations of the church are growing up in this unclean soil.

Let me digress for a minute and talk about soil, or "the land," as the Bible refers to nations. Part of the reason I penned these pages is that I believe God is crying out for a clean nation to rise up and reclaim our unclean culture.

In Jeremiah 3:1, we read, "'If a man divorces his wife and she leaves him and marries another man, should he return to her again? Would not the land be completely defiled? But you have lived as a prostitute with many lovers—would you now return to me?' declares the LORD."

And in verse 9 we read, "Because Israel's immorality mattered so little to her, she defiled the land and committed adultery with stone and wood." These verses allude to the fact that the immorality of the people affects God's perspective of the land. I want to take you even further through this principle, and explore how our sexuality affects God's view of a land or a nation.

Leviticus probably isn't a book you spend a lot of time in, but there are some real jewels in its pages. In chapter 18 you will find listed all the sex acts God disapproves of. In short, God says to only have sex with your wife. Verses 24 and 25 say, "Do not defile yourselves in any of these ways, because this is how the nations that I am going to drive out before you became defiled. Even the land was defiled; so I punished it for its sin, and the land vomited out its inhabitants."

God commands them not to be sexually immoral, because this is how the land became defiled or unclean. Then he says something really interesting. As the people are immoral, "the land" will vomit them out.

To reiterate his point to the Israelites that their sexuality determines whether or not a land is defiled or unclean, he says in verse 28, "And if you defile the land, it will vomit you out as it vomited out the nations that were before you." The consequences of making a land unclean is that they would get kicked out of the land God wanted to give them.

Most men or pastors I share this with have never heard that God looks at a land as clean or unclean based upon sexuality. This truth was verified several times as Israel was forced to leave the physical land that they defiled in this manner.

Sometimes, I feel we Christians are being kicked out of our American culture. Our God has been taken out of our schools, and his commandments have been taken out of our courthouses. Even his nativity scenes have been removed from some public places. I don't know about you, but it feels as though we are being kicked out of our own land.

Consider each of these questions for a moment.

- If God were to look at America based upon its sexual immorality, especially its leadership in sexual immorality, what would God say? Unclean or clean?
- If God were to look at your state or your city based on its sexual morality, would he say unclean or clean?
- What if God were to look at your local church— remember, he sees all—what would he have to conclude? Unclean or clean?
- If he were to look at your life based upon your sexuality alone, what would he conclude? Unclean or clean? You already know the answer.

I thank God for the blood of Jesus who paid for all my sins. Because of Jesus, God considers all of us as blood-bought men. I want God to be able to look at every man, church, city, state, and nation and declare us clean, smiling upon us all.

Your Destiny Is Waiting

In the previous chapter we saw the impact sexuality has on a nation's destiny. In this chapter I want to show you specifically how our sexuality has a direct impact on our personal destinies.

There is a direct connection between your sexual behavior and your destiny in Christ. God has designed you and me to do amazing things for his kingdom, and our level of sexual purity will determine how useful we are. Sex and destiny are linked. This is why the devil works so hard to ensnare you in sexual sin. His goal is to neutralize you through immoral sexual behavior, thereby making you ineffective for the kingdom. And after twenty years of counseling men on this issue, I can tell you this is evidence that the devil is scared of you. Yes, afraid. Here's why.

We have all seen great men of God excelling in the Lord and moving toward global impact, only to succumb to sexual sin. Suddenly, all they can do is watch as their ministries, families, and reputations crumble in shame. Had these men prepared themselves to fight against sexual sin—been transparent with others, sought counsel, remained accountable—we would still benefit from their ministries today.

As I like to say about the devil, if he can *seduce* you, he can *reduce* you. There are examples of this throughout the Bible, especially regarding sexual temptation. Our biblical forefathers' and mothers' responses to temptation had a direct impact on their fates. Just look at Joseph's response to Potiphar's wife, for example, in Genesis 39:7–10:

> And after a while his master's wife took notice of Joseph and said, "Come to bed with me!" But he refused. "With me in charge," he told her, "my master does not concern himself with anything in the house; everything he owns he has entrusted to my care. No one is greater in this house than I am. My master has withheld nothing from me except you, because you are his wife. How then could I do such a wicked thing and sin against God?" And though she spoke to Joseph day after day, he refused to go to bed with her or even be with her.

Joseph said no and stood his ground. His response cost him his job and almost his life. He was thrown in jail, but he refused to compromise his integrity for a moment of pleasure. You are probably familiar with the rest of Joseph's story. He interpreted dreams for Pharaoh, then in a single day he went from an imprisoned man with sexual integrity to being the second highest leader in the greatest nation in the world.

Had Joseph failed this test, he could have easily been disqualified or killed earlier in his life after Potiphar found out about it. That one sin would have caused the death of millions by famine, because he would not have been where God needed him to be in order to interpret Pharaoh's dreams and tell him to store crops for food. Sexual purity is what maintained Joseph's destiny.

The same is true of many other great men in the Bible, such as Moses, Daniel, and Elijah. However, Samson's life took a very different turn. God loved Samson and placed a calling on his life, as Judges 13:24–25 points out: "The woman gave birth to a boy and named him Samson. He grew and the LORD blessed him, and the Spirit of the LORD began to stir him while he was in Mahaneh Dan, between Zorah and Eshtaol."

But Samson had one problem, and her name was Delilah. "Some time later, he fell in love with a woman in the Valley of Sorek whose name was Delilah" (Judges 16:4).

You are probably familiar with Samson's story. He told the secret of his strength to Delilah, and she used it against him to have him captured and blinded by the Philistines. His destiny was limited because of his sexuality. God gave him a final victory when he pushed down the temple pillars, killing more Philistines in his death than he did during his entire life. His life could have been even greater, however, if Samson had used his God-given strength to lead and protect, providing an example for us all. We can only wonder what Samson's life might have looked like had he lived for his true destiny.

What about you? What's it going to be? Will you fight and take a stand? Or will you give in and forfeit the Lord's calling on your life?

The devil tried to stop me through a series of emotional setbacks. My father and mother abandoned me at an early age. I fell into the traps of sexual abuse, drug addiction, pornography, and promiscuous sex. Looking back, I can see that the devil was rightfully concerned that I would figure out God's purpose for my life and pursue my calling in the Lord. Thankfully I did. By God's grace I was able to recognize the wonderful life he had planned for me, which caused me to give up all my addictions and give everything back to him. As a result, I have seen God gradually increase my influence through major media outlets and through a robust international speaking platform. I now see men saved and set free from sexual sin everywhere I go.

And that's my point. Your freedom isn't just about you.

Your destiny is tied to the destiny of others—all around the world. People are desperate for answers, and once they find out how shallow and unsatisfying a life of sin is, they will want the real thing—Jesus. I believe it is God's desire to expand your influence for his kingdom. He can make it happen if you will remain faithful.

Now is the time to get clean. Your family, friends, church, and even nations are waiting for you. I could give you hundreds of examples of men caught up in pornography, adultery, and other improper sexual behaviors who decided to repent, become accountable, and build a support team. As a result, they began to help others and change the world.

You are God's solution for someone or something on this earth. He lives in you, and he has given you special gifts unique to your personality. You are a great warrior, and the enemy attempts to scar warriors early in life. Beyond your guilt, shame, or desperation is a heroic, epic story only you and God can write.

I love it when I get to speak to teenagers. I see a world of destiny in their young eyes, and yet their generation is under blistering media assault. They face enormous peer pressure and temptation when it comes to sex. So when I get the chance to talk to them, I often say, "When you feel tempted by someone, tell that person they are simply too small for you." Which means that the moment of pleasure the person is offering is too small compared to the great destiny that is ahead of them. The truth is their destinies are much bigger than a moment of pleasure. Moses knew this and made the right choice at the right time. The Bible refers to his decision in the book of Hebrews:

> By faith Moses, when he had grown up, refused to be known as the son of Pharaoh's daughter. He chose to be mistreated along with the people of God rather than to enjoy the pleasures of sin for a short time. He regarded disgrace for the sake of Christ as of greater value than the treasures of Egypt, because he was looking ahead to his reward. (11:24–26)

Moses knew he was a son of the great King, and he willingly gave up the pleasures of this world. The same is true of you. God has called you to his service. Don't compromise your destiny by viewing pornography or living a promiscuous lifestyle. Those actions are simply too small for you. You are not called to peck the ground like a domesticated chicken waiting for slaughter. You are like an eagle destined to fly to incredible heights! If need be, humble yourself so others can be free.

Authority at Stake

In the last two decades, the sexualization of our culture has grown exponentially. Never before in the world's history has so much explicit material been available to so many people. The devil has moved the porn store from the "bad" side of town directly to your cell phone. When it comes to corrupting the church of Jesus Christ, the enemy will stop at nothing.

Why has this battle so intensified that anyone watching television will be sexually assaulted, or slimed, within minutes of turning on the tube? Why do we celebrate sexual humor, suggestive language, open adultery, and fornication? And why are so many Christian men watching it? These are important questions to ask. If a man wants to comprehend the pit he is in and the work it is going to take to become clean, he must understand why. While I was in Bible college

and seminary, I knew and understood the reason for obeying God and helping people; therefore I could endure final
exams, long nights, and challenging professors.

Knowing the reason for staying clean will have a similar
effect on you. It will give you strength in the fight for sexual
purity. It is easy to swim with the current in our present culture, but it takes real strength and courage to swim against it.

Let me take a step back in time and share something
with you that forever changed my perspective. A while
back, I was quietly reading the Scriptures, when something
amazing happened. A verse suddenly jumped out at me.
You know what I mean—one of those moments when time
stands still and it appears as if the words are alive, coming
off the page. I became so excited I had to get up and walk
around. I blurted out, "Oh wow, God! This is good! This is
amazing." I already had several degrees in theology, so I felt
as if I knew every Scripture there was on sexual immorality. But this was different. I was now seeing exactly what
the enemy was after with every person and church—and he
could only get it through sexual compromise.

This revolutionary verse is found in Revelation chapter
2, where Jesus is speaking to the seven churches. I think it
will tell you something that might come as a surprise. (I'll
give you a hint, sexual temptation has absolutely nothing to
do with sex at all!)

The apostle John was known for his love for Jesus. In

fact, some might argue John had the closest relationship to the Lord of all the disciples or apostles. If this is true, then it is no wonder Jesus trusted John with perhaps the greatest revelation ever given to man. And remember, throughout this entire section of Scripture, Jesus is speaking after the crucifixion in his permanent resurrected state as the Son of God. Addressing the seven churches, Jesus directed John:

> To the angel of the church in Thyatira write: These are the words of the Son of God, whose eyes are like blazing fire and whose feet are like burnished bronze. I know your deeds, your love and faith, your service and perseverance, and that you are now doing more than you did at first. (Revelation 2:18–19)

The opening of this letter is the easy part. Jesus praises the church for the positive things it is being and doing. The Lord repeats this pattern of opening each letter with encouraging words throughout this section of Scripture. Ironically, praise is crucial to recovery. It instills hope. Most men who struggle sexually have hidden their secret lives of sin for so long that they are hounded by a tremendous fear of being found out. If their fears come true, they may fall into a pit of despair. By contrast, it is the Lord's nature to be gentle with his people, even when they are in sin. He truly is longsuffering. As the second chapter in Romans points out, "Or do you show contempt for the riches of his kindness, tolerance and patience, not realizing that God's kindness leads you toward repentance?" (2:4).

By offering praise, Jesus gently affirms his love for them. He continued to John in Revelation, "Nevertheless, I have this against you: You tolerate that woman Jezebel, who calls herself a prophetess. By her teaching she misleads my servants into sexual immorality and the eating of food sacrificed to idols" (2:20).

The Lord now transitions into the real issue. First, notice the use of the word *tolerate*. It appears this church knew what was going on but just looked the other way. Were the leaders merely putting up with open immorality? Not only that, but the woman somehow worked her way into a position of authority—a self-made leader.

This situation isn't unique to the first century. We see the same thing happening today. Many pastors refuse to believe that the men, women, and youth in their churches are viewing pornography and engaging in immoral sexual behaviors. Either they simply don't want to believe it or they are trapped by the same problems and feel a lack of credibility to address those who are in the wrong.

Today, the word *tolerance* is used as if it were a great virtue. I want to dispel this myth. No doubt God is patient, and we are all living proof of his patience. However, God is not tolerant in that he is consistent in what he does and doesn't like in our behaviors and hearts. Otherwise Jesus would not have had to die for the sin of the world. The same things that upset him in Genesis upset him throughout Scripture. Remember, "Jesus Christ is the same yesterday and today and forever" (Hebrews 13:8).

God does not tolerate sexual sin. He never has and he never will. And there are plenty of good reasons for it. This particular sin is very harmful on several levels. Not only does it destroy an individual's soul and spirit; it also is very difficult to erase. Once you have an affair, you can never undo it. It is a part of you forever. You can be forgiven, but you cannot erase past actions. This, of course, has dire effects on the family, causing divorce, child abandonment, and a whole host of other unintended consequences. And when the family breaks down, entire societies break down.

That is why we find Jesus still saying the same things in the last book of the Bible, after the resurrection, Pentecost, and years of church growth. He hasn't changed. Tolerance of this type of sin in our lives and in the local church is unacceptable.

Revelation 2:20 introduces the "woman Jezebel." The Lord is using a name from the Old Testament to describe this woman's character. The original Jezebel was introduced in

the book of 1 Kings as the wife of King Ahab. She had pro-
found influence and used it for evil. She quickly became the
most feared person in Israel. The Bible records several inci-
dents that made her infamous for evil deeds ranging from
false accusations to mass murder to assassination to forgery.
The name Jezebel is casually used as a woman who cheats,
is immoral or controlling. She derived her power from her
sexuality—she got all dolled up for Jehu even though he
killed her husband, King Ahab—and used it to dominate,
control, manipulate, and murder. From that one sin came
all the other evils that plagued Israel during her reign. One
result of her seduction was the massacre of the prophets of
the Lord. She even struck fear into Elijah's heart, one of the
most powerful prophets ever to walk the earth. In response,
she incited the full wrath of God for her complete rebellion.

How does this relate to sexual immorality today? Jezebel
hasn't changed. Her spirit has the same goal: seduce you,
then reduce you. If you are a child of God, she especially
hates you and your family. Believe me, she's not your friend.

So you say to yourself, "Hold on a minute, Doug. I'm not
that bad. I only looked at a few photos. I am not as bad as
other guys." Really? Do you think it matters if you look once
or twenty times? Let me ask you a question. Do you know
why a heroin dealer gives out free samples to a newcomer?
Because he knows if the person gets just one taste, that person will beg for more. Then he will have a customer for life.

Do you want to become a lifelong customer? If you think you can control lust, you are deceived. The opposite is true, and unless you can see this, it will only increase its hold on you.

Back in the book of Revelation, this newer Jezebel was most likely some kind of Sunday school teacher or cell-group leader in the church. It seems as if she was a Christian, not some cultural rock star perverting the people. After all, she was a member of the church and called herself a prophetess. She taught duplicity and compromise, a Jesus-and-immorality gospel. Her doctrine seems to have said that you could be a Christian and sleep around and do whatever you wanted to sexually. She certainly taught that individuals, not God, were in charge of their sexuality and they were free to do as they pleased. It appears, however, as if this Jezebel was still in the early stages of her teaching. Since the Lord knows there is only one end—destruction—to this kind of sin, he offered an olive branch. "I have given her time to repent of her immorality, but she is unwilling" (Revelation 2:21).

This verse demonstrates Jesus' incredible patience. Jesus gave her time to repent. Wow. The truth is, he does the same thing with us. The Holy Spirit convicts us of our sin repeatedly in the hopes that we will turn away from it. A sign of the Lord's mercy in our lives is the allotment of time to make a change. He doesn't come in with a heavy hand and demand we stop; rather, he comes to us gently and gives us room. This approach doesn't last forever, of course, but

isn't our God's generosity a beautiful thing? He is extend-
ing that same grace to you today. If you will be honest with
yourself, seek help, and get clean, God's blessing will return
in a great way to your life.

But in this woman's case, her heart was unwilling to
repent. She was saying in her heart, "No thanks. I'll do what
I want." Here is what I have discovered about unwillingness.
If we refuse to change, after repeated conviction of the Holy
Spirit, our hearts become hardened. We are now walking in
the opposite direction from God. Because he is our Father,
he will let us drift for a while before he takes action. By that
time, his actions may include temporary pain or humiliation in order to get our attention. In all of this, his real goal
is to bring us home so we can be long-term friends.

I am glad God is patient with each of us and walks
alongside us, even in the sexual areas of our lives. I am also
glad that, as a Father, he is willing to bring us to a place of
willingness again so we can repent of our deception. But
here is what happens if we don't: "So I will cast her on a bed
of suffering, and I will make those who commit adultery
with her suffer intensely, unless they repent of her ways"
(Revelation 2:22).

A bed of suffering does not sound so good to me, especially when Jesus is the one making the bed. I tell the men
who attend my conferences that the devil has to guess how
to hurt us, but God doesn't. He knows exactly what will

create pain for us. If we are God's children, he most likely has "spanked" us for wrong behaviors at some point in our lives. For some it was pride, and for others fear or flat-out rebellion. But this bed of suffering is a spanking on steroids!

For more than two decades now, I have talked to men with all types of sexual sins and addictions. I have the rare opportunity to watch God work on both sides of his conviction. When people repent, grace is given, and rarely are there significant consequences in their lives. If they refuse, however, the discipline often leads to disgrace and sometimes public exposure. The result of refusing is tremendous pain for that person and often for those who love him.

When God has to discipline someone because of his continued hard heart, things can get really ugly. I have heard of many creative ways God has exposed a man in secret sin. Let me list a few, just to give you an idea of what lengths God will go to love a man who is trapped in an unclean lifestyle.

- Terry was looking at homosexual pornography and printing it off at work. For "some reason" the printer stopped working but held its file. Then the office printer kicked in a little while later and the pictures started printing where they left off. The IT department was called in to investigate and tracked it to his computer. He was fired, he called his wife, and she ended up divorcing him. Talk about a bad day.

- Paul was making a phone call to set up his appointment with a prostitute and didn't realize his wife was "somehow" conferenced in on the call. He had an angry welcome when he got home.

- Stan, after having several sexual affairs, started a new one. The first time Stan had sex with his new partner, she got pregnant. He was blackmailed for years until his legal counsel told him to tell his wife. When he did, she divorced him.

- Marc, a top executive, had several affairs. He engaged in one affair for several months with a young employee. She sued Marc and the company for sexual harassment for several hundred thousand dollars.

- Eric thought he was real cool when he was running around on his wife while out of town. He attended a party with another woman and didn't know someone took a picture of them kissing and placed it on a Facebook page. A friend of his wife came across this photo, and Eric had to face the music.

- Tim was cruising for a prostitute and picked up a cop instead. He was arrested, and the arrest was printed in the paper. Tim was a pastor. His job ended that day.

- Carl, a doctor, was flirting on the Internet with a teenage girl he'd never met. Over a period of months they become sexual in their conversations and Carl set up a time to meet this girl at a local mall. He sat down, started talking to her, and was soon surrounded by cops. Carl is now sitting in jail.

- Juan, also a doctor, had several affairs, including one with a patient. As the affair started to deteriorate, as they always do, she contacted his medical board. Juan will be losing his license for a while, which will affect his family for years.

I think you get the idea. A bed of suffering is not the place any man wants to find himself. Suffering hurts.

If you notice in the second part of that verse in Revelation, the Lord says, "And I will make those who commit adultery with her suffer intensely unless they repent of her ways" (2:22). I love the word *unless*. Even in this letter, God was reaching out to those in adultery and asking them to repent so he wouldn't have to bring suffering into their lives. Jesus really prefers our voluntary repentance to discipline. During my years of counseling, I have never heard a man or woman who committed adultery say they would do it again. From where I sit, the act itself creates so much suffering, guilt, shame, and double-mindedness that the adulterer would give everything he or she possesses to take it all back.

I am a Jesus guy. I know he died for all sin and will immediately forgive a repentant heart. The stubborn will encounter long-term consequences, however, such as STDs, pregnancies outside of wedlock, lawsuits, job loss, or removal from ministry for a season. And that's not all. "I will strike her children dead. Then all the churches will know that I am he who searches hearts and minds, and I will repay each of you according to your deeds" (Revelation 2:23).

This is a powerful verse. Jesus is very straightforward here. He will visit the sins of the fathers on their children. Jesus' intent is that, if necessary, this discipline would clarify to all the churches that he is Lord of the church and this flagrant disobedience in leading others into disobedience is intolerable. When he says he repays us according to our deeds, he is staying true to his character. This is reminiscent of the parable he told in Matthew 25:32 about separating sheep from goats, sinners from the godly. He upped the stakes, and the church leadership in Thyatira was faced with a decision:

> Now I say to the rest of you in Thyatira, to you who do not hold to her teaching and have not learned Satan's so-called deep secrets (I will not impose any other burden on you): Only to hold on to what you have until I come. (Revelation 2:24–25)

There are men and women in every church who are the real deal. They are sexually pure before marriage and in marriage. There are ministers of the gospel who are also pure and have no sexual issues whatsoever. I am so glad there are men and women like this. On the other hand, I have seen male and female ministry leaders who were fully sexually addicted. They were cheating and lying to their spouses and ministry partners, yet after they repented, they were fully healed. Today they live sexually pure lives. I have observed firsthand how God can translate sickness into glorious health. And Jesus won't miss a beat.

Satan's deep "secret" is quite simple: be immoral. He has used this same trick throughout the centuries, but it's not a secret anymore. Anytime you're being tempted into immorality or viewing pornography, you are falling for the enemy's teaching hook, line, and sinker. Anytime you are following the path of sexual purity, you are following the Spirit and teaching of our God. It is that simple. After men come clean from this fog, the simplicity of the truth of sexual purity becomes clear and self-evident once again.

We are finally at the best part of this letter in Revelation, the verse that turned my world upside down and fueled my desire to stay sexually pure. I have walked you through some challenging Scriptures up until now. But here is the payoff. "To him who overcomes and does my will to the end, I will give authority over the nations—" (Revelation 2:26).

This Scripture promises that if we overcome the duplicity of sexual immorality, God says, "I will." He doesn't say, "maybe," or "I might." He says, "I will." When God says, "I will," he keeps his word. Period. When God says he will give you authority over the nations, he will. Notice he did not say authority just in your home, your city, state, or country— but "over the nations."

You only have to look back at our last chapter to see God keep his word. He did it for Joseph; he made him a leader who influenced several nations. He did it for Esther, who kept herself pure. Purity allowed her to become the queen of the most powerful empire. We see it in Daniel's life, and in so many lives over church and world history.

You may not be a global political figure, but you can have international influence on those you impact. Giving to missions, using your gifts or talents to help others or even contributing through a helpful website you create can minister to others all over the world. Over the decades, God has given me international influence through television, radio, books, conferences and in the lives of men globally who have already been impacted by the teachings in this book. God will decide how he will use you to influence. You decide if you are clean and ready for him to do his glorious will within you.

Do you now see what this battle is really about? It is not about sex at all; it is about your destiny to rule and reign with Christ. I know this Scripture is true. I am living it, and God keeps expanding what he is doing to help more people globally. You are no different. You are God's warrior on earth. Your destiny is waiting.

4

Carry Your Weapons

I am sitting in my office with a client who flew in for an emergency three-day intensive with me. His life is a mess. I will call him Joe, but of course that's not his real name.

Joe is a bright guy when it comes to business. He started a company and grew it up to employ several hundred people. Joe is athletic and almost fifty, but he looks forty. He is married to Karolyn, an equal in every way. She is bright, hardworking, godly, fit, and very attractive.

Joe has had a problem with sexual sin on and off throughout his marriage. He, like so many men, has a history of porn and masturbation several times a week since adolescence, so he definitely has landmines worked into his brain. His particular landmines are twenty-year-old blonds, and they are usually the type he employs.

Joe crossed the line and committed adultery three

times earlier in his marriage. He and his wife, Karolyn, went to a local Christian counselor and thought they had dealt with Joe's infidelity. They worked on their marriage; Karolyn forgave Joe and gave her heart back to him, thinking all was well again. The problem was that Joe gradually walked the familiar road to failure that so many other men have traveled. Joe gradually began to lust after and flirt with the twenty-year-old blond women in his workplace. He also started to rationalize that he could masturbate again. He reactivated his landmines over a couple of years.

At first, Joe's flirtatious behavior was sporadic, sometimes months in between; however, over time, his flirtatious behaviors became more consistent. The behavior continued to increase until he was fully back to weekly self-gratification and fantasy, including pornography, which he readily found on his new phone that accessed the Internet.

Joe didn't feel he needed to tell Karolyn any of this because he justified he wasn't cheating. He also justified that the flirting was all in fun, so he didn't think this was anything he needed to be honest about. Joe was back to having a secret world, and the walls of that world were slowly getting thicker through Joe's participation and sexual reinforcement of the images he was attaching himself to both neurologically and emotionally.

Then it happened. Stupidity meets opportunity. A

thirty-year-old blond single mom started to return Joe's flirtatious behavior with increased intensity. Joe leveraged his position of employer, created time for them to work together, and pursued and engaged in a sexual relationship with his employee. Joe thought he was living a great double life again. He was feeling all the highs of a new sexual romantic relationship. He was texting, calling, and e-mailing back and forth on the business computers. Joe thought, once again, he was a real man, until he got caught.

Let me digress for a moment, and then I will get back to Joe's story. Really, when it comes to marrying one of God's daughters, I'm not sure what some guys are thinking. Marrying God's daughter is marrying the apple of God's eye. Many of you reading this know exactly what I mean. If you have a little girl, you know she has a special place in your heart. You don't want any pain to come into her life. Your desire to protect her is strong; it can bring out the papa bear in you really quickly if you think there is a threat of danger to her.

If you and I, who have a fallen nature, have so much love that it creates protection toward our daughters, then how much more would a perfect, all-knowing, all-powerful God feel toward his daughter, your wife. I hope you realize that when you marry God's daughter, as I point out in my book *The Miracle of Marriage*, that means God is not just your Father but he is also your Father-in-law. He sees everything and knows even the things in your heart and mind. We all do well to realize that we have a Father-in-law God.

Now let's go back to Joe's story and the event that was about to change his life. Remember the single-mom employee whom Joe was cheating with and all the elation he was feeling? All that went away as he was being served papers accusing him of sexual harassment. Joe didn't see any of this coming. He had been intoxicating himself with lust secretly for years. This allowed him to operate in the dark until everything came out into the light, and yet one of the worst moments of Joe's life was still to come later that day.

Joe had to go home and face a woman he had already cheated on in the past, who forgave him for his past behavior and loved him. He would now rip her heart out, stomp on it one more time, and this time his reckless behavior also threatened their business's survival and reputation.

Joe had no choice. His lawyer said as a co-owner his wife had to know; there was no way to keep this a secret. So Joe walked toward his unsuspecting wife, who had a nice dinner waiting and was happy to see him. Joe must have looked like death, because her first question was to ask Joe if he was sick. He told her no, but they needed to talk.

Joe and Karolyn sat down and he began to tell her a slightly sanitized story about his relationship with another woman. As I mentioned earlier, Karolyn was a bright woman.

She knew he was not telling the whole truth. She asked, "Did you have sex with her?" Joe dodged the question, only to be hit directly with the question again, but at such an intense level he felt compelled to honestly answer, "Yes."

At that point Karolyn broke. I mean really broke. She was crying, screaming, convulsing on the floor. This went on for a couple of hours, and then she asked him to leave. As he was headed for a hotel, Joe realized that all in one day he lost his fantasy world, his lover betrayed him, his business was threatened, and he had devastated his wife again. She had been so good to him for decades, and he had quite possibly lost his marriage.

Why did all this hell break out in Joe's life? He dropped his weapon! I believe that part of every man's role in life is to be a protector. Throughout history, men have created weapons as symbols of protection—from bows and arrows, swords, guns, and tanks to fighter jets. Men have always protected with weapons. God gives you various weapons to protect yourself and those you love. These weapons include the fear of the Lord, wisdom, the Word of God, accountability, honesty with your spiritual authorities and spouse, porn blockers, and accountability software. So many weapons are at your disposal.

Here is the limitation of these weapons: they can only go in one direction at a time. In other words, your protective gear or weapons, like Joe's, is either facing the enemy or it's facing those you say you love. Now I don't think any man sits down and says, "I want to aim my weapons toward my family. I want to emotionally bludgeon my precious wife, sons, or daughters. I want to destroy trust and create immense pain in my life and theirs." Yet, this is exactly what has happened to Joe, his wife, and family.

You and I need to aim our protective gear and weapons against the enemy's plan for our lives, so we don't one day become the perpetrator of this crime of lying, cheating, and hurting those we love.

Before I go further, I want to discuss a principle from James 1:15. The translation will differ, but the principle is the same. The King James Bible states, "Then when lust hath conceived, it bringeth forth sin: and sin, when it is finished, bringeth forth death."

The main thought here is the principle of the seed. Lust is a seed because it produces fruit. Seeds are the only things that can produce a fruit. Seeds can only produce the fruit of their DNA. For example, a tomato seed doesn't produce pumpkins; it can only produce tomatoes. The DNA of a seed is powerful, and with proper nourishment will be unstoppable in becoming what it is determined it shall be.

Now let's go back to Adam's creation for a moment. From what was Adam created? That's right, dust or dirt. All of us men folk are fancy dirt. Dirt is where seeds are planted. Lust is a seed; it's a seed with a known DNA and ultimately can create death in a man's life. The first stage of sin is lust, which can be described as those long looks, double takes, rubber necking, and overevaluating when a woman is in your field of vision.

Women are three-dimensional creatures with spirits, souls, and bodies, with relationships, responsibilities, and dreams for their lives. When we lust, we remove all these other aspects of their beings and just look at their packaging, or their bodies. We objectify or make them things, instead of souls or people. In lust, we devalue the amazing soul that a woman is and make her into a lust hit—entertainment that we scan into our brains.

Lust is absolutely wrong. Who says so? God does. In Exodus 20:17, otherwise known as the Tenth Commandment, God clearly states, "You shall not covet your neighbor's house. You shall not covet your neighbor's wife, or his manservant or maidservant, his ox or donkey, or anything that belongs to your neighbor."

It's clear we are not to lust after our neighbors' wives. You might think, *Great! My five neighbors are not attractive to me, so no problem.* But when Jesus was asked about who our neighbors are, he responded and made it pretty clear that *everyone* is our neighbor (Luke 10). That means that we are not to lust after *any* woman on planet Earth. Paul said to treat "older women as mothers, and younger women as sisters, with absolute purity" (1 Timothy 5:2). Why sisters?

Because that puts a relationship context around each person. Most of us would not lust after our own physical sister regardless of her level of attractiveness, because, of course, she is our sister. In the absence of the option to lust, we see her as a whole person with feelings, a history, relationships and value, not as an object.

Lust, if it is not destroyed at this level, can and will grow. And if it is watered repeatedly with more lust, fantasy, and pornography, lust will continue to grow and become stronger. If you masturbate to lust-inducing pictures, it's like feeding super-fertilizer to the seed, or genetically engineering it. If you lust after the same person repeatedly, you are in real danger of creating a situation where you will be drawn toward her. You are reinforcing that situation with your lust, as Joe did with blond employees. Because he lusted after blond women when he masturbated, this specific targeting led Joe to be attracted to the blond employee who eventually sued him.

The second stage of the seed of lust is sin. The sin can start off small, like inappropriate humor, jokes, asking about a woman's marriage or telling her how bad your marriage is, a hug, a longer hug, private meetings, and then kissing, sex, and ongoing sex. Sin is the evidence that you have fertilized lust over time. Since sin is the next growth stage of lust, it doesn't just happen; there is always a process of nurturing the seed of lust.

You can repent of sin, be forgiven, and once again grow spiritually, although there may be consequences of sin that continue for quite some time. If a man chooses not to repent, however, he is guaranteed only one future, and that is the fruit of lust and sin: death.

A man may lust for years, never thinking he will sin. I have heard that hundreds of times from men, Christian men, who thought they would never cross the line. They didn't understand that feeding lust guarantees the seed will grow into its next stage. Whether a man is saved or not, that's the principle of the seed.

Sin can also be fertilized. By repeating the porn, masturbation, secret sexual chatting, texting, or cheating, you fertilize lust and sin. This reinforcement promotes the growth of this sin in your life, making lust and sin stronger and stronger over the years or decades. Sin, like a plant that has sprung up from the ground, definitely grows in a particular season (Hebrews 11:25). *Season* is an interesting term to use because it is a period of time with a beginning and an end. A man in the season of sin often believes he will never get caught; he thinks he is smarter than those other guys. This man is deceived, because there is absolutely no such thing as a secret; there is just a season of secrets. Countless men learn this the hard way. If a man doesn't humble himself before God and others during this season of sin, he will be faced with the seed of lust reaching its final fruit, death.

This harvest season of death has its own distinct beginning. It starts with the humiliation of getting exposed or caught.

As I began to describe earlier, I can't tell you the countless ways God has contrived his sons-in-law into getting caught. It's the guy who makes a phone call to a prostitute and somehow his wife is accidently conferenced in on the call. It's the voice mail, text, or e-mail that is found. It's the call from the husband of the other woman, who has repented in her season of sin. It's the accidental Facebook post that a friend or relative came across, that shows you and the blond woman together. It's the wife showing up to surprise you at your hotel during a "business trip" and walking in on you unexpectedly. God is creative and specific when the season of death starts.

In the beginning of the season of death, a man can still repent. Sometimes there is restoration, and sometimes there is death. Death can have many faces, such as not seeing your grandchildren because your children don't want to be around you. Death can include not being able to walk your daughter down the aisle on her wedding day, no longer being called Dad, your calls not being returned, a photograph from your ex-wife's wedding to her new husband, the children calling her new husband Dad, the cost of a career or license, public humiliation in a newspaper or broadcast, living alone and going further into your sin, or adding other addictions, even facing jail time for child porn on your computer. Death has many faces, but death hurts everyone you love. Those you love are forced to deal with you now being a perpetrator of pain instead of their protector.

Let's talk about the characteristics of a man who is a perpetrator of pain and doesn't protect his family versus those of a man who protects his family by using his weapons against the enemy.

A Potential Perpetrator of Pain

1. A man who has the potential to perpetrate pain never committed to be clean in the first place.

As men who live in a very perverted world to a greater extent than any other generation before us, where Christians can carry porn stores on their cell phones all day, often without any blocks or accountability, we have to commit to being clean to be successful. The man who will be vulnerable to dropping all God's weapons for him is the one who never really assessed the battle ground he is in, and his place in that battle. If a man doesn't perceive the battle he is in, he is more likely to fail, causing pain to himself and those he loves.

This man has never—or never completely—committed in his heart to be clean. Much like the man who never commits to having a retirement, he lives life unaware that he will be broke because he didn't intentionally plan to care for himself or his family.

Some men have never been guided into a moment with God and with other men in which they declare they will become and stay clean sexually. They may not even know what it entails. If you're a single man, being clean is about self-control, freedom from porn, and it's about how you date women. If you are married, being clean means being faithful and satisfied with the wife God gave you. No man is worthy of a wife; she is a gift.

In this war, the naive pay the heaviest price. If you haven't purposed to be clean when temptation comes—and I said *when*, not *if*—you can be truly caught off guard, and with little strength, or support, you may fail unnecessarily.

If you haven't committed to sexual purity, take a moment and pray a prayer similar to this one:

> Lord, you saved me—all of me. I declare and commit in my heart to be clean sexually. Forgive me of all my sexual sin. I receive your death as full payment for my past. I commit all my sexuality, my eyes, heart, and sex organ to obey only you. I am committed to do all it takes to stay sexually clean. Thank you for all you have done to help me stay clean all the days of my life, in Jesus' name. Amen.

If you prayed this prayer, or one like this, then tell another man that you have purposed to be sexually clean all your life, and have him pray in agreement with you about your commitment.

2. A man who has the potential to perpetrate pain has no plan.

Men who have the potential to perpetrate pain not only have no commitment to sexual purity as we just discussed, they have no plan. They didn't see a need to think through ideas that could help them stay clean. You know the old saying, "If you don't know where you're going, any road will get you there."

The man without a plan is vulnerable. You could easily find yourself in a compromising situation with yourself, the Internet, Facebook or another social network, work or a social situation, or on the road. Then, *whamo*! Opportunity to sin meets an ill-prepared man, and the inevitable happens. If you want an example, read Proverbs 7:7–23, a story about a simple young man who meets a prostitute, and it costs him dearly. We will talk about practical plans later in this chapter and this book.

3. A man who has the potential to perpetrate pain has no boundaries.

One of the easiest ways to find out the state of a man's weapons is by looking at his boundaries. A man who is more likely to drop his weapons has no boundaries or very weak ones. He reads worldly material and watches sexuality in all forms of innuendos and scenarios on television. He doesn't mind occasional, partial, or full nudity on television or in magazines.

He accidentally or intentionally can be hit by sexual material and not think twice about it. He has no boundaries regarding talking to other women about their unhappy marriages or sex lives, and no limitations on sexual humor, flirting, or other inappropriate conversations. He hasn't thought through what's acceptable to talk about with women, whether they are single or married.

Unknowingly, those men, like Lot in the Old Testament, are vexing their souls. Second Peter 2:7–8 says, "and if he rescued Lot, a righteous man, who was distressed by the depraved conduct of the lawless (for that righteous man, living among them day after day, was tormented in his righteous soul by the lawless deeds he saw and heard)." Notice that simply seeing and hearing unrighteousness, such as what we experience in the media, tortures our Christian soul. Lot didn't technically do anything wrong; he just beheld and listened to the sexual world on a regular basis. A man with no boundaries will be greatly challenged to desire to stay clean.

4. A man who has the potential to perpetrate pain is not honest or accountable.

Your weapons will drop here for sure. When you keep your sexual conversations, behaviors, pornography, or masturbation a secret, you are in agreement with darkness. You cannot kill something you embrace. When you start lying, your weapons are protecting lust and sin. Men protect what they love. When you protect lust and your sexual sin, your weapons are dropped toward the enemy and can actually start facing those you are called to protect. It's similar to someone you may have seen in the movies. He starts by protecting what is right, but gets influenced or seduced to the dark side. He drops his weapon for what's right and over time actually starts defending the dark lord and is now using his sword against those he once protected. So first you drop your weapon, then listen to the enemy, and lastly protect the enemy.

A lack of accountability is always a sign of a man whose weapons are down. This, combined with sexual independence—the attitude of I own my own sexuality, not God or my wife—is a big tip-off. He hasn't taken advantage of a porn blocker program like Covenant Eyes for phone and computer accountability, nor does he have an Internet activity report sent to an accountability partner. He is alone in the web of pornography called the Internet. A man in this defenseless position is easily accessible to the enemy of his soul and his family, and extremely vulnerable to sexual temptation and acting out. It's almost like telling the devil to take his best shot.

Most of us don't want to be that warrior not using his God-given weapons. You, I hope, want to be a man who not only keeps himself clean but also protects his family and his brothers and leaves the legacy of a clean life. You deserve to be a clean man. Following are some characteristics of men who have their weapons facing the enemy, alert like Gideon's men at the water (Judges 7).

1. Men who protect are armed and ready to commit to be clean.

A man aiming his weapons the right direction will have made a specific commitment to be clean. While speaking at singles and youth conferences, I often have young men and women come to the altar to commit their sexuality to Christ. Why do that? It gives them at least one point in time where they have consciously made a commitment to live a clean life. That moment, that physical separating from the crowd, regardless of past mistakes, gives them the anchor of having at least made a decision. This action is similar to what you did if you said the prayer just a few pages ago and told someone. You have committed to be clean.

The Bible says, "For as he thinketh in his heart, so is he" (Proverbs 23:7 KJV). As a psychologist, I know we are the sum of our commitments and the discipline to keep them. As a man, if I commit to something, I will attract the people and things I need to fulfill that commitment. When a man makes a commitment, he is immediately confronted with distractions from keeping it. My son and daughter are both commitment-type people. When they decide to go for something, be it football, cheerleading, debate team, or Tae Kwon Do, they are totally in, and that immediately pushes other things to a much lower priority.

When men commit to a clean sexual life, it attracts people, ideas, and strategies, such as accountability software, accountability partners, support groups, and resource materials to help them stay clean. The commitment in your heart already may be the reason God brings these people and resources into your life. Your clean commitment clears your vision, and you will begin to see threats clearly as well. Prepare for them, and enjoy victory and a clean conscience after winning those battles.

2. Men who protect have a plan.

When you carry weapons with you, it's easy to remember you are at war. The enemy is taking out a large number of our men and our male Christian leaders in this war. I remember having to fly out of town after my pastor fell because of sexual impurity. I sat on the plane with the proverbial napkin and wrote down the names of my pastors and their wives who had fallen specifically to sexual sin. I counted exactly 50 percent of my pastors or their wives who fell publicly to this attack.

I can't say it enough: this is a war on our sexuality and our families! Warriors should have a plan for staying pure in their various environments. Let's start at a warrior's home.

The Internet is selectively blocked because he doesn't want a porn store attacking him or his family. There are clear boundaries and accountability around the cell phone and Facebook (real warriors have little time for this anyway). Accountability software reports are sent to his wife and accountability partner.

He has a plan for work—whom he can go to lunch with and appropriate boundaries for conversations. He has a plan for when he or his spouse travels. He has a plan for the opposite sex in general regarding hugs, touching, and praise. He even has a proactive plan for entertainment—television, magazines, movies. He is thinking ahead of the devil, not thinking about what he can get away with but rather how he can get away from the world's filth.

3. Men who are armed and ready are honest and accountable.

A plan is great only if it is implemented. A couple who plans to have a million dollars in the bank when they retire at sixty is admirable. But if they never follow the plan or have others keep them accountable, they will have only created a plan and not reached their desired dream. It takes discipline every month to arrive at that dream.

A man whose sword is protecting himself and those he loves is honest and accountable. He still lives in an environment of temptation, as we all do. But if he opens an e-mail and sees something inappropriate, he tells somebody immediately. He cooperates with his wife in telling her the things she wants to know, and he has a trusted man or men to confess any inappropriate thoughts to as well.

Let me give you an example. I was exhausted after three days in Canada speaking at a men's and marriage conference and doing professional training for Christian counselors on sexual addiction. I got on my plane and took out my tablet to write a chapter of a book. The woman sitting next to me reached into her bag and began to pull out a magazine. All I could see was the red letter *P*. I instantly knew it was going to be a *Playboy* magazine.

I looked the other way and sat facing the bathroom. I was angry. I prayed in my spirit, "Lord, if she'll put it away, I'll witness to her." I didn't have an "accident" and look; I stayed focused. She put her magazine back in her bag, went to the bathroom, and when she came out she pulled an everyday magazine out of her bag. I tried to share, but she seemed more comfortable with silence. When I got off the plane, I immediately called my accountability partner and my wife. I hadn't seen anything inappropriate; I just didn't want to be slimed by her issues.

When you're at war, you utilize the weapons of honesty and accountability. A man who has a commitment and a plan for this is much more likely to be successful. If he drops his weapons at a lust level, and then gets honest and accountable, then he is really less likely to drop it on the sin level. He would have to choose to lie to get that far down the road.

Here is an idea that can literally quash inappropriate behaviors for those who struggle. Some men don't mind being honest about the occasional, or even regular slip of lust, porn, or masturbation, but they don't stop these behaviors. They do what I call "puke and go," then continue to go back to the vomit of their unclean behavior (Proverbs 26:11).

The man in this situation may have a sex addiction or he may just need to put consequences in his life for his behaviors. Most guys struggle because of classical conditioning. That includes positive conditioning for a behavior. To change a behavior you might want to change your conditioning from positive rewards for lust to setting up a negative reward for this behavior. If you look at something or do something inappropriate, have a consequence set up and enforce it. A consequence is something that hurts you (negative reinforcement). Let me give you a list of suggestions.

- No media for one, two, or three weeks
- No cell phone for one, two, or three days
- Walk to work
- Pick up trash for two to four hours
- Give money to a political or nonprofit organization you really disagree with

- Eat a raw onion
- Run two miles (if you're not in shape)
- Eat Ben and Jerry's at 10:00 p.m. (if you are in shape)
- Leg lunges for half a mile or one mile

The consequence has to be painful to you. For example, if you love riding a Harley, it stays parked if you choose to drop your weapons. Share these consequences with your wife, accountability person, or group. If you do something requiring a consequence, then embrace the consequence.

I find that when men add a layer of consequences, especially those who have struggled in the past, it keeps their weapons facing the enemy. Men who have lost this battle for decades change into men who become winners and protectors of those they love, due to the humility of consequences.

You deserve to be clean your entire life. The fact you are reading these pages means you are most likely aware which way your sword is currently facing. Congratulations if you have a plan and are working to implement it. If you need to switch the direction of your sword, do so. Start with a commitment. Tell a man. Get accountable and honest.

God's Spirit is calling out to men in every nation to lift up their weapons and fight. He has called you to be the protector of those you love, not a perpetrator of pain. It's men who must protect their families, churches, and cultures. It's men in the last decades who have dropped their weapons, making our church impotent to address a culture getting sicker by the day.

Men are the solution God has chosen. When the world is in trouble, he sends a man. Listen to the call of God in your life. Look at your wife and children's faces or your future wife and children; their futures largely depend on you. Will you sacrifice them to stay unclean and indulge yourself in a little temporary pleasure as you fertilize lust, sin, and death?

I don't believe for a minute that you are that kind of a man-boy. I believe there is a man inside you who wants to look in your wife's—or future wife's—and children's eyes, and from the deepest part of your being, with every cell in your body, say the word *clean*! As you lift your weapons and fight the good fight, fight to win. Be the patriarch of blessing and purity, as God has ordained you to be.

Remember, it's not your battle scars or even the lost battles that count; it's about winning the war. Our God is calling us to be his solution for the condition of this unclean world. Aim your weapons in a way to honor God and our families, and let's take back our land.

U + P = D

I use a formula to help explain a very important cause-and-effect relationship. Not only is this formula statistically verifiable; I have seen the real faces and hearts of men, women, and children whom this formula has negatively impacted over the course of my counseling career.

The formula is: U + P = D. Let me decode this for you. *U* is a short way to say "you." *P* is a short way to say "porn or pornography or any other sexually inappropriate behavior." *D* is short for "destruction." The longhand version of this formula reads, "You plus Pornography (or other sexually inappropriate behavior) equals Destruction." Simple.

Fire is the best analogy for men who engage in ongoing and unchecked lust, fantasy, pornography, masturbation, and other sexual behaviors that are not relational with their wives. Fire is great. Mankind had benefited from, survived with, cooked over, and been warmed by contained fire for thousands of years. Today we have these wonderful creations in our houses called fireplaces.

A fire in containment, like a fireplace or a stone-lined campfire, is a beautiful thing. It is both safe and beautiful to watch. Another contained fire that many of us men love is a grill. I enjoy the fire in my grill because I can slap on an ordinary piece of meat, add some spices, and in short order I have a culinary masterpiece for my family to enjoy.

Fire in a contained environment is a gift. Fire in an uncontained situation, however, can wreak significant damage. Again, you plus uncontained fire equals destruction ($U + P = D$). I live in the Western part of the country, where there are wildfires almost every summer. These fires either escaped from their containment because they were neglected or had no containment to begin with. A wildfire grows and grows and consumes everything in its path. It can consume a forest, the plains, houses, and even human lives if they're in the way.

Sexuality is like fire in many respects. First, fire and sex are gifts to be enjoyed only in contained situations. The only containment for sex and sexual appreciation of a woman is marriage. Sex within a marriage is amazing, comforting, invigorating, and deeply satisfying if it is relational. Our wives alone are God's perfect sexual will for our lives. I tell my wife, Lisa, that I know when we make love I am in

God's perfect will for my life because she is his only will for me sexually.

Unfortunately, some men sin and do not contain their sexual fire to their wives. Their sexual fire strays into areas of self-indulgence, lust, fantasy, pornography, masturbation, flirting, grooming, and sexually engaging with other women. Sexual fire that leaves the confines of the fireplace, so to speak, has consequences.

Most men don't experience the consequences immediately, so they don't believe there will be any. They continue day after day, year after year, not realizing that their lives are being consumed. They are losing thousands of hours of time; allowing their spiritual, emotional, and moral souls to be stunted; and having their worth destroyed by the fire of their sexual lust and all its manifestations.

That's only the beginning of this fire's consuming damage. I have talked to thousands of couples in whose relationships the man's lust and sexual behavior had burned out of control. One man was a prominent pastor. His behavior remained secret for years. When it became public, the consequences largely affected his wife and children. Years later, some of his children remain damaged, and this man had honestly believed his behavior wouldn't hurt anyone. His choices damaged his church, a very prominent church in his city, and thousands left the community.

This church experienced a significant decline in size

and global impact. Months after this event occurred, I was speaking in Europe at an international conference and met people from this congregation who were still significantly hurt and confused by this man's sexual choices outside marriage. This one man's decision continues to affect his church, missionaries, his city, and many other areas of the world.

No man should experience this type of negative consequence in his own life, his family's lives, and others' lives, even those around the globe. I want every man to have a clean life—one with a good effect on the world around him. A lifetime of encouraging others in the Christian life is an amazing gift to have and enjoy, and it is worth fighting for.

You and I have seen men who have a clean life and leave a positive legacy. We have also seen or heard about men who have fallen. Now I want to take you deeper into studying the impact of a man who chooses an unclean lifestyle on those he loves.

For the next several pages I want to share with you statistically, not anecdotally, the impact of a man's secret unclean life on his wife and his children, and the real-life impact of $U + P = D$. These statistics come from two of my books relating to sexual addiction. In *Partners: Healing from His Addiction*,[1] we conducted two studies of sexual addicts' spouses. The first study included eighty-five spouses, and the second included thirty-nine spouses, who answered questions about the impact of their husbands' secret sexual addictions on their lives.

Beyond the Bedroom: Healing for Adult Children of Sex Addicts[2] addresses what happens to sexual addicts' adult children. Sometime during childhood, these subjects became aware of their parent's inappropriate sexual behavior. The statistics represent the impact on their lives from their fathers' or mothers' poor sexual choices.

Effects on the Spouse

When a man chooses an unclean lifestyle of secret lust, pornography, or other sexually inappropriate behaviors, he might think that what his wife doesn't know won't hurt her. Nothing is further from the truth.

As Christians, we believe when we get married, two become one. God's final creation in the garden was marriage. Yet our bodies are not only one with our wives but one with the Lord as well. Not only does God grieve because of what we men choose to do to ourselves, I believe he grieves because of what men's secret lives do to his daughters—our wives.

Let's start off by seeing how the women surveyed in *Partners: Healing from His Addiction* (Discovery Press, 2011) rated their self-esteem before their marriage to a man with an unclean life.

Prior to my relationship I had:	
25%	High Self-esteem
40%	Average Self-esteem
27%	Low Self-esteem
8%	Very Low Self-esteem

I want you to keep those numbers in mind for a moment. Let me show you how they rated their self-worth during their relationship with a man having a secret life.[3]

During my relationship with the sex addict, I felt my self-worth was:	
5%	High Self-esteem
20%	Average Self-esteem
38%	Low Self-esteem
37%	Very Low Self-esteem

As you can see, there are major differences in a woman's self-esteem after being in a relationship with a man with a secret sexual life. Here is another way of looking at those numbers.

Difference in Self-Esteem			
	Before	During	Difference
High	25%	5%	-20%
Average	40%	20%	-20%
Low	27%	38%	+9%
Very low	8%	37%	+29%

Most of us men would like our wives to feel good about themselves. We want our spouses to feel confident, beautiful, and adequate. If you are dabbling with a secret sexual life, you are almost guaranteeing your wife's self-esteem will be damaged.

There's another significant way a sexually unclean life can change your wife. I asked eighty-five women to tell us whether they had struggled with depression before their relationships with their sexually addicted husbands. A total of 39 percent said yes, they did struggle with depression prior to their relationships; and 61 percent said no, they did not struggle with depression.

And 82 percent of these women stated they struggled with depression during their relationships with the sexually addicted men. These men more than doubled the depression rate in their wives, which is significant.[4]

Following are the symptoms of depression and the percentages of women who claimed to have each symptom during their relationship with a sexual addict.

Symptoms of Depression	
74%	Poor appetite or overeating
78%	Unable to sleep or oversleeping
82%	Low energy or fatigue
71%	Feelings of restlessness or being slowed down
69%	Poor concentration or difficulty making decisions
78%	Feelings of hopelessness
33%	Suicidal thoughts
82%	Depressed mood
62%	Diminished interest or pleasure in most activities[5]

It is interesting that living with a sexual addict also affects a wife's preoccupation with food. Prior to their unhealthy relationships, 40 percent stated they struggled with some type of eating disorder. During their relationships with these men with secret lives, that number went up to 62 percent. Of the ladies who stated they struggled with eating disorders, 84 percent said overeating was an issue, 5 percent said they had bulimia, and 11 percent claimed anorexia.

Before we go any further with the effects a secret sexual life has on a wife, let's recap. If you are having a secret sexual life, your wife's self-esteem is going to go down significantly; she is very likely to suffer several symptoms of depression; and if she turns to food, she will gain significant weight due to your choices. Would you like to feel bad about yourself, be depressed, and experience weight gain because of a secret behavior your wife chose to take part in on an ongoing basis, and that you absolutely know is not God's will for her life? Probably not. I don't think it's very fair for a man to inflict this and other symptoms on his wife just so he can look at porn, masturbate, and be sexually inappropriate.

Following is a quick list of other behaviors these women have reported. Remember, many of these behaviors are results of living with a man with a secret sexual life.

Wives' Behaviors

85%	Checking up on him
78%	Being controlling
76%	Looking for more proof
68%	Feeling threatened or insecure around other women when with the addict
58%	Not having sex or being hypersexual
66%	Reinforcing fears of abandonment
65%	Trying to think about what he might be thinking about
61%	Sarcasm
58%	Scoping out women he might be looking at
54%	Raging
52%	Shaming him
47%	Pretending it's a perfect relationship
46%	Fantasizing about him acting out[6]

Effects on Children

Others whom you love very much who are significantly affected by your sexual behavior are your children. These statistics are from my book *Beyond the Bedroom: Healing for Adult Children of Sex Addicts*. Respondents ranged from twenty-one to sixty-one years of age. Of these, 95 percent had a dad who was a sex addict.

When asked at what age they found out about their parents' inappropriate sexual behaviors, this is how they responded on the survey.

Age of Discovery	
8%	before 5
36%	6–10
15%	11–15
8%	16–18
5%	19–25
0%	26–30
13%	31–40
13%	41–50
2%	51 or above

The survey revealed that 67 percent found out about their dad's or mom's inappropriate sexual behavior before they left the house at eighteen years old.

These adult children of sexual addicts were asked how they found out about their parents' inappropriate sexual behaviors. Following are their responses.

How children discovered their parents' sexual addictions:	
7.5%	Parents confessed to child
11%	Parents involved child in keeping the secret about their addiction
48%	Child found something that involved their parent's addiction
7.5%	The other parent told child
4%	A family member other than a parent told child
22%	Other

We also asked these adult children about their fathers' behaviors of which they were specifically aware. Remember, most of these adult children knew this information about their fathers before they left the house.

Witnessed Behaviors	
39%	Pornography
26%	Multiple affairs
20%	Masturbation
8%	Prostitutes
4%	One-time affair
3%	Homosexual behavior

Following is a list of areas in the subjects' lives affected by parents', mostly fathers', sexual addictions.

Areas of Impact on Children's Lives	
81%	Self-esteem
79%	Spirituality
71%	Social life
71%	Dating

70%	Emotional life
69%	My marital relationship
67%	Morality
64%	My romantic relationships
64%	My sexual beliefs
64%	My sexual addiction
62%	Depression
57%	My sexual choices
45%	Financial situation
41%	My parenting
38%	Eating disorder
17%	My sexual anorexia (avoiding intimacy and sexuality in marriage)

Following are more statistics regarding negative effects of the subjects' parents' secret sexual lives.

Felt Damage of Parents' Sexual Addictions

94%	Had difficulty trusting others
91%	Had difficulty in emotional intimacy with their spouse and others
89%	Was suspicious of others and others' intentions
86%	Had difficulty knowing their real selves
81%	Had difficulty finding true spiritual congruency
82%	Believed themselves to be of less worth than others
79%	Had difficulty expressing their feelings
76%	Found safety in stuff or objects

This is not just my opinion or some theory. These answers remove the deception that pornography and a secret sexual life don't have an effect on other people. An unclean or secret sexual life *does* have a significant impact on the ones you love.

Remember the formula U + P = D? I want to share with you man-to-man what I have seen in my office week after week. It exposes the truth of that sad equation over and over again. I have sat in my chair while a husband first discloses to his spouse that he has cheated on her, whether with a prostitute, another man, her best friend, or with porn during the entire marriage, and worse behaviors than I can write. I have seen the invisible lightning bolt hit her—spirit, soul, and body. I have watched as hundreds of women convulsed in pain and cried hysterically, and some looked and felt as though they momentarily went insane.

I have talked to hundreds of children from age six to adulthood who wonder why they weren't good enough for their dads to stop this behavior. Why did their dads abandon them and raise some other woman's children? I have worked with women and men who realized, after years of terrible decisions, they were looking for their parents' love in some bizarre way.

While counseling for decades, I have seen unclean sexual lives cause an astonishing array of carnage. In light of this, I am earnestly praying for you men to join the many others who humbled themselves and got and stayed clean. I see miracles every week: a real man stops his inappropriate behaviors, stops sacrificing his family for his secrets, and on a daily basis fights for himself to stay clean so he can enjoy the privilege of being a husband and a father. As men, your lives have an influence. Paul said we are living epistles (2 Corinthians 3:3). We are the message of the gospel to our families and friends.

Let me give you another formula: $U + C = L$. The letter U is short for "you." C is short for "clean"—that's you living these principles and having a clean life for the rest of your life. L is short for life or life-giving. When you live a clean life, you also have an incredible influence, but this time a positive one. I have seen this formula play out many times. I have known godly men who stayed true to their God, true to their wives, and true to their children. They were imperfect, but their families could trust them as husbands and fathers. These men left a legacy of perseverance, patience, and character. Their children were proud to have had them as their dads, and the men's lives inspired them all in some way.

I have also seen the resurrection story recreated here. It's a story where a man starts his life with the formula $U + P = D$, and then changes somewhere along the way to $U + C = L$. These men often also experience their wives coming to respect them over time, trusting them again. Their children can rebuild their faith and learn to trust in Dad and others through their own healing process.

You decide the kind of influence you have. My prayer is that each ripple from the impact of your life has the echo of clean.

6

Clean Brain

The war over lust is multidimensional. In this war to be clean, you have several battlefronts. I want to show you how to sharpen your skills in a battle you may not even know you are in. This is a surprise for most men. Worse yet, this is often a battle most men have created, when it could have easily been prevented.

I need to take you back on a personal journey. It started more than thirty years ago when I was in Bible school. God would impress upon me to read certain scriptures. But when I would read one particular verse, I didn't understand its meaning. Then God would impress this same scripture upon me again and again and again, even though I still couldn't understand it. This went on for many years, from Bible school through seminary and then after graduation. I discussed the verse with my theology and philosophy professors because it contradicted the teaching that all sins are the same. One day, as I was doing research on sex and our brains, God revealed its meaning, and it truly was sweeter than honey. It was a revelation I will never forget.

That scripture was 1 Corinthians 6:18: "Flee from sexual immorality. All other sins a man commits are outside of his body, but he who sins sexually sins against his own body."

I really couldn't wrap my head around why it was that when we sin sexually we sin against our own bodies. Why didn't the Scripture state that when we lie, cheat, steal, or any other host of sins we sin against our own bodies? Why is sexual sin different?

Remember, I was seeking answers in Bible school and seminary. In those fine institutions, they gave us all kinds of Bible aids and even tortured me with Greek and Hebrew. I took this verse apart in so many ways. I remember looking up this word *body* in the Greek, thinking it would unlock some mystery and end this game of peek-a-boo. Do you know what the Greek word for *body* really meant in the original language? You guessed it: *body*. It really just meant our physical bodies, not our souls, spirits, or anything else. This verse stayed a mystery.

I believe science confirms Scripture. The field of neuroscience was gaining its wisdom during these years as well. Around the time I was researching the brain and sex because

I was working with sexual addicts, I found the missing piece to what God was trying to show me.

Your Sexual Brain

The brain, being the second most important sex organ for men, is something every man needs to understand if he is to have a clean life. The brain is an amazing machine; and when it comes to sex, that's absolutely no different. For journal support and all the technical information and references, go to the American Association for Sex Addiction Therapy's website at www.aasat.org and order the DVD *Biological Sex Addict*.[1]

Your brain is the pleasure center for your body, especially when you have a sexual release. When you release sexually, your brain receives the chemical mother lode of endogenous opiates. These opiates are the single highest chemical reward for anything you can ever do. You can run and work out, but sex is by far the biggest chemical high we get in life.

Most men have experienced this high, regardless if it was sex with their wives, with themselves through pornography, or through immorality with another person. Sex feels good; dare I say, *really* good!

God in his merciful design of our bodies created what I like to call sexual imprinting. This sexual imprinting is a

biochemical program that strongly connects and bonds you
to whomever or whatever you are viewing at the time you
have a sexual release. This is the most powerful connection
and attachment you will have in your life.

God hoped we would follow his commands regarding sex so we would never struggle with lust of others. If
you wait until marriage to have sex, including not viewing
pornography, you sexually bond and connect only to your
wife. You will not crave others; you will only crave her. Most
men, however, including myself, did not know about or did
not follow God's commands sexually. We, therefore, have to
deal with some consequences.

Our brain cannot separate reality, fantasy, and pornography. Neuroimaging has shown us that our brain lights up
the same way, whether we view a real object or imagine that
same object. Let's suppose your brain has a supercharged
Web browser connected to it. Every time you masturbate,
you hit a certain Web page. Each time you hit this page—say,
a certain type of woman or sex act—the browser records it
and places it at the top of the search page results. Every time
your brain thinks about sex, it goes to the top of the search
page, and you desire that the most; then the next entry
down, and so on. With this technique you actually create
an attraction to anything or anyone—real or imaginary.

Let's suppose you use your brain this way from age fifteen until age twenty-five. You would have a mega attraction

to the unreal, self-created, self-worshiping world of lust. You would have created many attractions, misconceptions, and false realities that simply may not exist in the real world, and then encouraged these false beliefs with the highest chemical reward. These become your landmines in the future. If you masturbated to exclusively blonds and marry a brunette, you could be unsatisfied because of the blond landmine you set up in your brain. If you preferred a particular sex act in your pornography or fantasy world, this could also be a landmine. You have set yourself up for failure because your wife is not a sexual actress and may not enjoy or even desire that particular sex act.

The Web pages you viewed are all connected to your brain. The more you view a certain image, the stronger that particular landmine is going to be. Some of these landmines are physical features of the woman or image you created or looked at during a sexual release. Some landmines are attitudes or emotions you projected onto the image; you may have received them from the image, such as a feeling of being wanted or being in control. These landmines, which are imprinted neurologically through biochemistry, are 100 percent your doing and not your spouse's fault.[2]

They may be the people or ideas you struggle with the most when trying to live a clean life. If you are moving along fine in your recovery and then, *boom*, you get hit by a thought, an image, or a fantasy, this is often due to one of those landmines. If you are feeling an attraction to a specific woman, this can also be a symptom of a landmine. Following is an example.

If a young man reinforces, through masturbation, sexual images of women of a certain race, he may have bonded to this race of women hundreds or thousands of times. When he is in the presence of a woman of this particular race, he will feel attracted to her beyond what he would feel toward a woman of a different race. He will often sexualize this particular race of women and may read more into a kind gesture, regardless of how innocent it actually was. I recently talked with a man who did exactly this. He is an international businessman married to an attractive Caucasian woman. He began viewing porn from another country. Over time, he ended up hiring prostitutes of only this race, and even had an affair with a woman of this race. He worked diligently on his recovery and visited my office to take his annual polygraph. He told me that after being clean for many years, he really loves and enjoys only his wife. His test verified his clean life.

But it's not just visual associations that cause trouble. Emotional landmines can be created as well. These are started by emotional or psychological themes that may have been utilized during a sexual fantasy or pornography use. For example, a young man engaged in a fantasy that included a woman using dirty talk. If he meets a real woman, regardless of what she looks like, who participates in dirty jokes or dirty language, he will feel a strong attraction to her and may be prone to sexualize her. He set up his own landmine, and then he is triggered.

These landmines are created by you and stored in your brain. When a person, a fantasy, or an image is similar to someone in the real world, or you interpret them in that light, you can be neurologically or emotionally triggered by that person. If you have a specific trigger, you can become very astute to the type of person that you have conditioned yourself toward. Many men have a wide variety of triggers that include both physical and emotional features, so they can be triggered by their environment on a regular basis.

Now let's go back to the brain. Step one: you create a high chemical reward when you release sexually. Step two: you bond or connect to that image or person. This bond is long term, not just immediate. Step three: your body stores this bond, and you are attracted to that person and image in reality or fantasy. You create a landmine. Step four: your environment or fantasy world can recreate this landmine and, *whamo*, you are flooded with feelings toward an innocent person or image.

When you sin sexually, your body stores these things for better or for worse. When you sin by engaging in sexual behaviors without your wife, you sin against your own body.

Some of you have also set up a similar attachment to

a fantasy person who looks like your wife. The fantasy has the same face and body, but often the fantasy wife is, let's say, more amorous or more creative than your wife. You can become frustrated when your wife doesn't measure up to the fantasy you created. I never recommend that married men masturbate to their wives because it can cause problems. When I travel, I make sure I come home regularly so I never sin against my body in this manner.

Don't worry. I can hear some of you thinking, *Doc, I'm already messed up, so now what do I do?* Trust me, I know what it's like to carry around a defective brain that has been rewarded for lust. I also have had a clean brain for more than twenty years and have helped many men clean up their brains too. Now we'll talk about how this happens.

Spank the Dog

Here is a principle I have been sharing with men for more than two decades. I mentioned this technique in my book *The Final Freedom: Pioneering Sexual Addiction Recovery.*[3] I call it, "Spank the Dog." This will be familiar to anyone who has had a puppy.

When I was a child, we had many dogs, and when they were puppies we trained them to go outside by first using newspaper laid out for them. Back in the seventies, my parents' philosophy on training dogs was that if a puppy would urinate on the carpet or anywhere that wasn't a designated area, they would spank the dog with a rolled-up newspaper (reasonably) and show them the place they were meant to go. Within a very short period of time using this negative reinforcement, the puppy would associate urinating anywhere except the designated area with pain. The dog wanted to avoid the pain, so it would stop urinating anywhere else.

To use this as an analogy for lust, the only designated place for your sexuality is with your wife. Currently you may be getting rewarded for lusting, fantasizing, or using pornography. That is called positive reinforcement.

I want to provide you with a tool that can also help you eliminate an unclean brain, and in a short time help you toward a clean life. Many years ago we did an informal study of two thousand sex addicts. We asked an open-ended question and gave no answers to pick from but requested that they write in their answers. We asked what had been most helpful in their sex-addiction recovery. The top answer was their wife staying with them. The second answer was a technique we teach in our office. If it can help a sex addict, it can help any man get a clean mind.

Get a rubber band and place it around your wrist for at least thirty days. Every time you lust, objectify, double take, rubber neck, or have a past image hit your brain, snap the rubber band. You will be amazed at how much of the time your brain is actually going the wrong way. Remember the dog: we are "spanking" your brain when it is going down the wrong direction.

Men have told me over the years that this negative reinforcement has shut down as much as 80 percent of their lust life and reduced the power of their landmines within a month. Some men have found it helpful to quote a Scripture after they snap the rubber band. This is like showing the dog where to urinate. Choose a Scripture, and after you snap the band, either say it out loud or in your head.

Here are some examples of Scripture verses that have been helpful in refocusing men's attention and healing their brains.

- "[Treat] older women as mothers, and younger women as sisters, with absolute purity" (1 Timothy 5:2).
- "What shall we say, then? Shall we go on sinning so that grace may increase?" (Romans 6:1).
- "Finally, brothers and sisters, whatever is true, whatever is noble, whatever is right, whatever is pure, whatever is lovely, whatever is admirable— if anything is excellent or praiseworthy—think about such things" (Philippians 4:8).
- "Therefore, I urge you, brothers, in view of God's mercy, to offer your bodies as a living sacrifice, holy and pleasing to God—this is your spiritual act

of worship. Do not conform to the pattern of this world, but be transformed by the renewing of your mind. Then you will be able to test and approve what God's will is—his good, pleasing and perfect will" (Romans 12:1–2).

The rubber band works. I have men also use it if their thoughts start ratcheting up, or during the change of seasons when women wear less and reveal more, or if they are going into a stimulating environment.

I also found that honesty works really well. If you have an accountability partner, tell him what your landmines are so you are not fighting alone. If you don't have an accountability partner, get one. The enemy of your soul looks for easy prey. The easiest prey for our enemy is a man who is not honest or accountable; in other words, he is alone. If you are not huddled up, you are an easy mark for the enemy. All natural predators look for the animal that has strayed from the herd. The freest men know that the cleanest lives are those men who have accountability in their lives. Be honest and get accountable so your brain doesn't get the best of you.

Proactively being honest in the heat of a battle is essential to staying clean each day. When lust hits, be it a landmine or some other opportunity in your environment, immediately call someone and tell that person what's happening. Honesty can be as simple as having Covenant Eyes accountability software on your phone and computer. When your wife, pastor, or accountability partner gets the report on your Internet travels, this is a form of honesty that can protect and help you lead and maintain a clean life. As soon as you call or contact your partner, you've prevented that landmine trigger or opportunity from taking you down the path of guilt and shame again.

You deserve a clean brain, but it doesn't come easy. You trained your flesh to lust after a certain image or emotional trigger. Unfortunately, your flesh doesn't change overnight. Be persistent, and over time you can begin to look at any woman as a person and not as an object. The longer you stay free from porn and masturbation, the easier it gets to see women as people.

"Braindar"

You have heard of radar. You know it sends out radio waves to identify the locations of objects. If you have trained your brain wrong, you could have a side effect called "braindar." This braindar can sense a trigger, image, shape, or color of hair before you make full visual contact with this person or image.

You may be walking in the mall when you see a poster. You can see the skin, but can't quite figure out if it's another Victoria Secret image. But your braindar has picked it up and you are not only aware, you also are getting a feeling in your chest—or somewhere else. This sense or feeling is your braindar. It's telling you there is a UFO in your environment. UFO is short for Unidentified Female Object. I know that women are amazing souls in incredible packaging and are not to be treated as objects. Guys know exactly what I mean when I say it's way too early to see the soul of that person when your braindar goes off. It will tell you only two things: its gender and its location.

If the braindar could talk, it would tell you something like this: "Female, questionable attire, at three o'clock." Believe it or not, this braindar can be a gift to you in obtaining a clean life.

In the past you used your braindar to locate a victim to lust after or worse. Now you can use your braindar as a warning device. You still receive the information of gender and location, but now it's all about what you do with that information. Instead of using the information to move toward the UFO, you use it to move away from the object. If the braindar says, "Object at three o'clock," then you look in any other direction so as to not include that UFO in your range of vision.

If you're at a restaurant or in another public place, sit away from the flow of the UFOs, or sit in such a way that you are no longer able to engage in a straight line with what your braindar has warned you about. If you are at an airport and you see a UFO sitting in a seat nearby, pick a seat where you are not able to look directly at her. I think you get the idea. Braindar can help you choose to move away from someone or something in your environment that can be stimulating you for whatever reason.

You can't control that you have braindar, but you can control how you use it. You can't control the environment, but you can control how you navigate your environment. Now let's leave the brain discussion and talk about some biblical truths that will inform your heart as you fight in this area.

Hating Well

We often are taught about how Jesus loved, taught, healed, or performed miracles. But have you ever thought about Jesus hating?

In Hebrews 1:8 and 9, the writer quotes Psalm 45:6 and 7:

> But about the Son he says, "Your throne, O God, will last for ever and ever, and righteousness will be the scepter of your kingdom. You have loved righteousness and hated wickedness; therefore God, your God, has set you above your companions by anointing you with the oil of joy."

Jesus not only loved righteousness, he hated wickedness. I believe there is a place in our hearts in which we need not to coddle our lust and sexual sin—we must hate it. We must hate it as the enemy it is.

Throughout my career, every day I have seen what lust eventually does to a man, his wife, and his family. If you could enter my brain and see the thousands of men crying about their mistakes; feeling fear and self-hatred; suffering losses of reputations, jobs, wealth, relationships with their children; and suffering loss of kingdom impact; it would make you nauseated. Then see the tears of godly women whose families have been destroyed, whose children are in pain, whose finances are destitute, whose bodies suffer from transmitted diseases, and who struggle with unhealthy habits caused by their husbands' lust. You could easily come to the place of hating lust, as I have over these past decades.

You will never destroy an enemy you embrace. As you clean your brain, it is helpful to hate lust in all its forms. Lust destroys everything and everyone around you. It can take your family and leave you appearing foolish. Hating this enemy can be an effective part of the process of achieving a truly clean brain and a truly clean life.

A Brain Covenant

There is one other tool that has been helpful for the men I counsel. We have been talking about the physical brain.

Now I want to switch to a way you can take your thoughts captive (2 Corinthians 10:5).

You may have read that we should be like Job and make a covenant with our eyes not to lust after a woman (Job 31:1). I am all for doing that; however, it's not the eyes that are the main problem. The main problem is what men are doing in their minds. A man might be looking at and maybe talking to a woman. Some guys have the dexterity to have a conversation and simultaneously have lustful thoughts, or even fantasies, about the person who is innocently talking with them.

I have come up with a technique that has helped men stop these thoughts from ever getting started. This can even be helpful in a situation where a man has to not only resist looking while talking to a woman who is inappropriately dressed but also doesn't want to have to deal with the sexual slime that can linger after such an encounter. I call this a "brain covenant." This is like a prayer you say at the beginning of every day.

It is very important you buy into the premise that it is every man's duty and calling to protect all women, at all times, in all circumstances. If you agree, then taking it one step further is easy.

Let's combine what I said earlier about the brain covenant with the idea of hating lust. If you pray early in the day, out loud and with conviction, a prayer that states a commitment to love women, protect them, and hate all lust toward them, it can be a powerful anchor of your commitment for your brain to follow and be aware of all day long. This prayer could go something like this:

> Lord Jesus, I am 100 percent committed to love all women today as your daughters and my sisters. I covenant with you to protect all women at all times, in every circumstance today, even in my mind. I hate lust of any kind of all women, and I covenant to protect them all this day.

What you are doing is anchoring your commitment to have a clean mind and a clean life. When you pray this daily, protecting women from your lust will become a lifestyle. You'll know this is true when you are successful in maintaining a woman's value regardless of how she values herself.

I hope you will take and apply these tools to have the clean life Christ has paid for you to have. Clean is who God made you! Clean is the way God thinks and feels about all his daughters. You will begin to see and feel how he does toward his daughters as you walk these principles out in your daily life.

Holy Hologram

When I was newly married to my precious Lisa, we would go on dates from Fort Worth over to Dallas. On one of these trips we strolled through a huge warehouse with many little unique shops. One of the shops sold holograms. I had never seen anything like them before. Unlike paintings or photographs, which are one-dimensional representations of an image, holograms are three-dimensional.

Inside these clear plastic cubes were three-dimensional images of a person's face, a car, a flower, or some other object. You could rotate the clear plastic cube in any direction and this image would stay three-dimensional. They were amazing.

If you are a Star Wars fan, you have seen a hologram. When Princess Leia wants to communicate with Obi-Wan Kenobi millions of light years away, she records a hologram of herself. When R2-D2 delivers the message, it's really impressive.

Let's talk about you and this three-dimensional holo-gram. You are at the very least a three-dimensional being. Paul wrote, "May God himself, the God of peace, sanctify you through and through. May your whole spirit, soul and body be kept blameless at the coming of our Lord Jesus Christ" (1 Thessalonians 5:23). This verse states that as a man you have a spirit, the part of you that understands and has intuition beyond just your brain. You also have an amazing soul, your mind, which processes faster than any computer and utilizes logic (at least most of the time). Your soul also composes your will. The human will is probably one of the strongest forces on earth. Our souls have emo-tions. Emotions are not truth; however, they provide a way to interact with God, others, and the environment. And you have a body. Some of you are in amazing shape. Some male bodies . . . well . . . there are all kinds of shapes. Whatever your body type is, it is unique to you.

I always thought it was odd that we were all so different in my family. My hair and eyes are such a dark brown they are almost black. My next sibling has lighter brown hair and eyes, the next red hair and blue eyes, and the last blond hair and lighter eyes. We are all amazingly different in hair and eye color.

Your spirit, soul, and body are just the tip of the iceberg of the amazing creation you are as a man. Let me expand a little. You are a man in *relationship*. You are in relationship as a son to your parents, possibly as a brother to a brother or sister. You have been in relationships with your neighbors and community throughout your life. You were, or still may be, a student in relationship with teachers and other students. You, at some point, had a relationship with God. You also have probably had relationships as an employee. You have probably had a variety of relationships with coworkers in different work environments. You may have had numerous romantic relationships. You have a unique sexual and financial history.

You probably also have had spiritual relationships with various clergy and church members. You have had fun together of various kinds, including vacations, sports, and creating. You may be single or married. If married you have the experience of marriage to another unique being. You may have children or grandchildren. You've probably had some amazing successes in life, and also some challenges.

My point is this: you are more than just another pretty face. For anyone to view you that way is what you might call photograph thinking. You are not a photograph, you are more like a hologram, multifaceted in every dimension. To see you as one-dimensional is to not see you at all.

I want you to see yourself as the multifaceted being you are, so you can see the hologram of each woman, too, instead of a one-dimensional face and body.

Every woman you see has a spirit. She is a spirit placed

in a body by God. She was uniquely created by God, she was created for God, and she will return to God at the end of her life. She has intuition, and by the firsthand reports from many women I've counseled, she can sense when she is being lusted after. Women have described being lusted after as feeling slimed by someone.

Every woman is an amazing soul. Her mind is full of information and wisdom. She has an amazing will that is utilized often in her life. She has an indefinable range of emotions that can be experienced by everyone she comes in contact with. She has an amazing and unique face, as well as body. She is beautiful, yet this is just a fraction of who she is. Just like you, she is much more than the three dimensions of spirit, soul, and body.

She is way more than her body parts or face, which is the box that many men try to put her into. She is a daughter of God whom it would take decades to get to know and understand. Seeing every woman as a hologram can be very helpful. A woman is more amazing than her packaging, and only a man who is willing to lay down his life for her in marriage will be fortunate enough to get the privilege of truly knowing her.

The next step of our discussion on becoming a holy hologram is to look at the "holy" part of this statement: our God is a *holy* God. Angels are described flying around heaven saying, "Holy, holy, holy is the LORD Almighty; the whole earth is full of his glory" (Isaiah 6:3). This is one of the most important aspects of our God.

When God created man in his image, I believe he created Adam and Eve with innate holiness. In their state of sinlessness, they were holy like any of God's creations until the fall. I also believe that our bodies are still innately holy. We were created by a holy God, and we were also created in his image according to Genesis 1:27. This image is innately holy.

Paul referred to our bodies as temples: "Do you not know that your body is a temple of the Holy Spirit, who is in you, whom you have received from God? You are not your own" (1 Corinthians 6:19). The temple is a holy place. Jesus referred to his own body as a temple: "Destroy this temple, and I will raise it again in three days" (John 2:19–20).

Consider that if our bodies and the bodies of women are holy, then the more body is exposed, the more holiness— fallen though it is—you are being exposed to. A woman's body is made only for her husband, who is to protect her; yet women's bodies are being fully exposed in pornography. It is this holiness and the perversion of this holiness that is so attractive to men.

Women are beautiful, but they are also holy!

In the privacy of their homes and offices or with their

cell phones, many Christian men intentionally look at a woman's nakedness. They are committing time and effort to lust after another woman. First, this is a problem because the Tenth Commandment tells us not to lust after our neighbor's wife. Yes, all women are our neighbors' wives. Next, let's take a look at Habakkuk 2:15 and 16:

> Woe to him who gives drink to his neighbors, pouring it from the wineskin till they are drunk, so that he can gaze on their naked bodies! You will be filled with shame instead of glory. Now it is your turn! Drink and be exposed! The cup from the LORD's right hand is coming around to you, and disgrace will cover your glory.

This is a powerful Scripture, but I have never heard it preached on. What the prophet was commenting on is commonplace today. The perpetrators of these condemned acts were committing time and resources to reduce these people to naked bodies and then look at them. What is more interesting is what Habakkuk says will happen to such a man. A man who intentionally goes around looking at nakedness will be filled with shame.

Looking at porn leaves you feeling dirty, defiled, separated, and left with a secret. This secret can make you feel concerned that one day it might be discovered. Many of you know exactly what I mean. I think our intuition is in sync with this scripture, knowing that one day our secret will be exposed.

The correct response to nakedness is to not pursue it and also to cover it up. Today that would be like having defense mechanisms like the ones we've discussed so far in this book, such as accountability software on our phones and computers, and pornography blockers in place to cover it up before we can get exposed to nakedness, or should I say to holy holograms.

If you are feeling guilt or shame at this point, know that's not the goal here. Jesus forgives us for intentionally looking at pornography. His blood is stronger than any sin, even sexual sin. I want to encourage you that a clean life is God's design for you, because he wants to bless your life.

So far, we can see that the body is innately holy. We also can see we have a responsibility to cover nakedness. Our hearts have drunk in the devil's perversion, and we can have one of two responses. We can protect holiness by covering nudity, or we can consume this holy nakedness in some sexual manner.

Let's examine a story in Genesis 18 that illustrates the two responses to holiness. Three men visited Abraham. When Abraham saw them, he hurried to meet them and bowed down. He fed them, and then the Lord told Abraham his plans to destroy Sodom, the surrounding city, because of its wickedness. Next is one of the greatest scenes of intercession ever recorded. Abraham asked God to spare Sodom.

Then the LORD said, "The outcry against Sodom and Gomorrah is so great and their sin so grievous that I will go down and see if what they have done is as bad as the outcry that has reached me. If not, I will know."

The men turned away and went toward Sodom, but Abraham remained standing before the LORD. Then Abraham approached him and said: "Will you sweep away the righteous with the wicked? What if there are fifty righteous people in the city? Will you really sweep it away and not spare the place for the sake of the fifty righteous people in it? Far be it from you to do such a thing—to kill the righteous with the wicked, treating the righteous and the wicked alike. Far be it from you! Will not the Judge of all the earth do right?"

The LORD said, "If I find fifty righteous people in the city of Sodom, I will spare the whole place for their sake."

Then Abraham spoke up again: "Now that I have been so bold as to speak to the Lord, though I am nothing but dust and ashes, what if the number of the righteous is five less than fifty? Will you destroy the whole city for lack of five people?"

"If I find forty-five there," he said, "I will not destroy it."

Once again he spoke to him, "What if only forty are found there?"

He said, "For the sake of forty, I will not do it."

Then he said, "May the Lord not be angry, but let me speak. What if only thirty can be found there?"

He answered, "I will not do it if I find thirty there."

Abraham said, "Now that I have been so bold as to speak to the Lord, what if only twenty can be found there?"

He said, "For the sake of twenty, I will not destroy it."

Then he said, "May the Lord not be angry, but let me speak just once more. What if only ten can be found there?"

He answered, "For the sake of ten, I will not destroy it."

When the LORD had finished speaking with Abraham, he left, and Abraham returned home.

That is my prayer as well. I pray God will raise up such a clean church that he will not have to address us as a nation. Please join with me in that prayer.

Two of these three visitors, the "men," then went down to Sodom. Starting in chapter 19, the Bible says that the two angels arrived in Sodom that evening. Now take a moment and think about all the people who have seen angels throughout Scripture, including Joshua, Isaiah, and Abraham. Almost always they are awestruck by them and their apparent holiness, and they fall on their faces. Lot was no different; his response to these holy angels was exactly like Abraham's, and he bowed down.

The angels must have somehow radiated something different than the ordinary person does. The angels were holy, and Lot's and Abraham's responses were very appropriate. You know the story: Lot insisted that the visitors come to his house and not sleep in the square, because Lot knew what happened in Sodom when darkness came.

> The two angels arrived at Sodom in the evening, and Lot was sitting in the gateway of the city. When he saw them, he got up to meet them and bowed down with his face to the ground.
>
> "My lords," he said, "please turn aside to your servant's house. You can wash your feet and spend the night and then go on your way early in the morning."
>
> "No," they answered, "we will spend the night in the square."
>
> But he insisted so strongly that they did go with him and entered his house. He prepared a meal for them, baking bread without yeast, and they ate.
>
> Before they had gone to bed, all the men from every part of the city of Sodom—both young and old— surrounded the house. They called to Lot, "Where are

the men who came to you tonight? Bring them out to us so that we can have sex with them."

Lot's reaction to holiness was to protect. The men in the town, however, were defiled by ongoing sexual perversions and saw the angels as something sexual to be consumed. The angels, being holy, brought out what was inside the hearts of the town's men. In their hearts, Abraham and Lot were moved to bow down, feed, and protect these holy angels. Abraham and Lot respected and had a desire to protect the angels' holiness. The hearts of Sodom's men were full of sexual sickness and perversion, and the holy angels exposed it.

Exposure to holiness brings out who we are. When you see the holiness of a naked woman, what's your reaction? Is it to protect and cover up her nakedness, as our God would want you to do, and you would feel better doing, since part of your calling is to be a protector? Or do you lust and desire to sexually consume the holiness of a naked woman? Making the wrong choice is guaranteed to result in shame and the dread of being exposed.

There is a clear illustration of the blessing or curse that comes from the response to nakedness. Most of you are familiar with the story of Noah and the ark. God commissioned Noah to build the ark, even though it had never rained before. Noah was ridiculed, but then it started to rain. The floods came and destroyed all mankind. After a while, Noah and his family found dry ground on top of a mountain and landed the ark. Noah planted a vineyard, and one night he got really drunk from the wine.

Noah was so drunk that he was lying naked in his tent. Here is a holy man of God, the man God spoke to and trusted to give humanity a second chance, and he is drunk and naked.

Noah had three sons: Ham (Canaan's father), Shem, and Japheth. Each one was faced with what to do with a naked father in his tent. Ham, first on the scene, didn't make the right choice. He beheld his father's nakedness. Other than tell his brothers, we don't know what Ham did.

Shem and Japheth had a different and respectful response to their dad's nakedness. They chose protect their father, not to entertain themselves. They instinctively did what Isaiah talked about—they covered his nakedness. They were so respectful they walked backward, so as not to see Noah's nakedness. They dropped a blanket over their father and walked out, probably feeling like they did the right thing. That's the clean life feeling you can have your entire life.

What happens next is one of the most intriguing stories in Scripture. "When Noah awoke from his wine and found out what his youngest son had done to him . . ." (Genesis 9:24). Again, we don't know what Ham did, but something made Noah pretty upset. Listen to what Noah spoke to Canaan, Ham's son: "Cursed be Canaan! The lowest of slaves will he be to his brothers" (v. 25).

Ham's inappropriate response to Noah's nakedness, whatever it was, caused Noah to curse Ham's son. I would never want to be the cause of a curse on my son, especially a curse on his productivity and ability to be promoted.

In naming my son, Jubal Lee, my purpose was to remind myself and him that, through Christ, his dad broke the sexual curses of our generation so that he could live free from them, and so far he has chosen freedom over bondage. It must have saddened Ham to know his inappropriate response to Noah's nakedness cursed his son and future generations.

Hosea also warns about our sexual behavior affecting our children. Hosea chapter 4 addresses how a father's sexual choices and behaviors affected his daughters.

> *"My people are destroyed from lack of knowledge.*
> *Because you have rejected knowledge,*
> *I also reject you as my priests;*
> *because you have ignored the law of your God,*
> *I also will ignore your children.*
> *The more the priests increased,*
> *the more they sinned against me;*
> *they exchanged their Glory for something disgraceful.*
> *They feed on the sins of my people*
> *and relish their wickedness.*

And it will be: Like people, like priests.
    I will punish both of them for their ways
    and repay them for their deeds.

"They will eat but not have enough;
    they will engage in prostitution but not increase,
because they have deserted the Lord
    to give themselves to prostitution,
to old wine and new
    which take away the understanding of my people.
They consult a wooden idol,
    and are answered by a stick of wood.
A spirit of prostitution leads them astray;
    they are unfaithful to their God.
They sacrifice on the mountaintops
    and burn offerings on the hills,
under oak, poplar and terebinth,
    where the shade is pleasant.
Therefore your daughters turn to prostitution
    and your daughters-in-law to adultery.

"I will not punish your daughters
    when they turn to prostitution,
nor your daughters-in-law
    when they commit adultery,
because the men themselves consort with harlots

> *and sacrifice with shrine prostitutes—*
> *a people without understanding will come to ruin!"*
> (vv. 6–14)

Knowing that there is even a slight chance that my sexual choices—pornography, masturbation, affairs, or prostitutes—could in some way affect my daughter and her future choices makes me want to run from these practices.

I also would like to believe that a man who chooses a clean life can have a positive impact on his daughters. I know my daughter has been positively influenced by my walking out of the room if something is inappropriate on television or in a movie. You do have an impact on your children's choices. Let's look at Noah's response to his two sons who respectfully reacted to his nakedness.

I love this! Scripture states, "He also said." God didn't end this story with the inappropriate response to nakedness and the resulting curse, but with the appropriate response of protection and the resulting blessings. Noah said, "Blessed be the LORD, the God of Shem! May Canaan be the slave of Shem. May God extend the territory of Japheth; may Japheth live in the tents of Shem and may Canaan be his slave" (Genesis 9:26).

Noah blessed Shem and Japheth. God's heart and design is that we would be blessed, that all we do would be expanded. He wants our response to the holy holograms of women and their nakedness to be that of masculine protection, not consumptive perversion.

The enemy knows God's heart is to bless us. That's why the enemy wants to tempt you into an improper response to lust, so that when you see a naked woman, you see her as a sexual object you can consume for self-pleasure. The enemy knows this displeases the Father. Remember, the enemy knew the Father before man was created.

So when you look at a woman, naked or clothed, know she is a holy hologram and a daughter of the Most High God. When she does face him, you want her to say that you protected her, and even if she was naked, that you looked away or didn't gawk at her on the Internet. You did not add to her suffering in any manner.

You are the protector of the holiness and nakedness of women because you are a man of God. You can have spiritual eyes to see holiness when you see a woman. As you walk in this clean life, you will be blessed. God loves to bless men who at any cost protect his holy daughters. If you have a daughter, how would you feel if you were sitting in a public place where someone was lusting after her? Or if a man was going out of his way to take inappropriate pictures of her and using them in a sexual manner? You would probably feel angry and disgusted.

Suppose that man was doing this at your daughter's apartment complex. Say there was another man who was a police officer and protected your daughter by having that man arrested. How would you feel toward the police officer? Probably grateful. You'd have respect for him because he protected your daughter. Even though he didn't know her, he did the right thing. That's how I want God to feel about all the men in the church—to respect them because they do the right thing when they see his daughters. When we cover and protect, we feel clean.

8

Really Under Authority

Many pastors have invited me to share the principles in this chapter with their churches. One pastor invited me to his church several times, which is not particularly unusual. But this was different because he kept having me come back to do the same men's conference over and over again. I became curious, since I typically do a wide variety of conferences at churches when I make repeat visits. After one such repeated conference, we were at lunch with several of his church leaders and his son-in-law around the table. I asked the question that had been on my mind: "Pastor, why do you continue to have me come back and do this same men's conference?"

He paused. I will never forget his approach to answering my question. He went around the table and asked each man how long they had been clean—meaning no masturbation or porn usage. Each man shared a similar response. They were clean from either my last visit to the church or from my visit before last.

Each man at the table was clean because he had been practicing the principles I have been sharing in this book. The pastor smiled, pleased with his men, and said, "That's why I continue to have you come back and talk to my men."

Men getting and staying clean excites ministry leaders and pastors. I am excited when I meet a man who introduces himself by saying, "Hi, Dr. Weiss. You don't know me. My name is _____, and I have been clean for two years. You saved my life. Thank you so much." This happens over and over again in restaurants, churches, and airports.

When you apply the principles in this chapter, in combination with the ones we've been discussing, I guarantee that you, too, can be well on your way to a clean life.

I love when the revelation God has shared with me also becomes revelation to another person through my work as a psychologist and my speaking engagements. These *ah-ha* moments are like idea popcorn that goes off in another man's spirit. I pray that as you read an account I have affectionately titled "The Three Owners," you have an *ah-ha* moment that not only becomes a revelation to you but also becomes a lifestyle to you as it has to me.

The Three Owners

I stand before hundreds and sometimes thousands of men, and their faces are absolutely dumbfounded as I explain to them that there are three owners of their sex organs (penises). I instantly see glazed-over eyes. In Texas the description is "like a cow looking at a new gate." I can almost hear their hearts and minds asking, *But it's mine! Who are the other two owners?* Then I say, "No, you are the third owner, not the first or second owner." This property doesn't totally belong to you.

American men have definitely bought a lie when it comes to their sex organs. Our culture tells us blatantly that your sex and sex organ totally, 100 percent, unquestionably belongs to you and only you. You are the captain of your sexual ship, king of your sex organ, as if it's an unalienable right like free speech.

Your sex organ does *not* belong only to you. Before we discuss more about the three owners, I want to lay down a principle so you can absorb this idea better.

Blessed or Cursed

Let's talk about the principle of blessed money or cursed money. Obviously, I hope you would want to have blessed money.

Malachi 3:6–12 is a good passage to study to determine

if someone is blessed or cursed financially. Keep in mind this was written to the people of God.

"I the LORD do not change. So you, O descendants of Jacob, are not destroyed. Ever since the time of your ancestors you have turned away from my decrees and have not kept them. Return to me, and I will return to you," says the LORD Almighty. "But you ask, 'How are we to return?' "Will a mere mortal rob God? Yet you rob me. "But you ask, 'How are we robbing you?' "In tithes and offerings. You are under a curse—your whole nation— because you are robbing me. Bring the whole tithe into the storehouse, that there may be food in my house. Test me in this," says the LORD Almighty, "and see if I will not throw open the floodgates of heaven and pour out so much blessing that you will not have room enough for it. I will prevent pests from devouring your crops, and the vines in your fields will not cast their fruit," says the LORD Almighty. "Then all the nations will call you blessed, for yours will be a delightful land," says the LORD Almighty.

I believe in tithing and believe everyone would be wise to tithe. My point is not about tithing, however, but about being under the authority of the Word of God. In this passage God is determining whether a person or a nation of people are blessed or cursed depending on their obedience. Their obedience to God's commands to tithe eventually blessed the individual and the nation with money beyond what they could imagine. Disobedience to God's command to tithe caused God to curse the money of those who didn't tithe.

As a side note, I meet with people who are in pain or in crisis within their lives or marriages. Over twenty years, I have asked Christian couples about the structure of their marriages, such as dating, spirituality, sexuality, sharing feelings, social life, and money. *Every* Christian couple who had significant financial troubles did not tithe. I also have multimillionaire friends who tithe abundantly.

If you are under authority and tithing, then your money is blessed. If you are not under authority by not tithing, then your money is cursed. My thought is, if you're going to have money, it might as well be blessed money.

The same is true of your sex organ. Since you have one, you can decide if it is going to be a blessing to your life or a curse, depending whether you are under authority or not. I love that we get to decide to be blessed!

Owner #1

The first owner of your sex organ is absolutely not you! You were totally bought by Christ Jesus as his slave. Many of you have memorized Romans 12:1 at some point: "Therefore, I urge you, brothers, in view of God's mercy, to offer your bodies as living sacrifices, holy and pleasing to God—this is your spiritual act of worship."

We are to offer our bodies—including our sex organs— as living sacrifices. All our sex organs are attached to and are part of our bodies. It's not as if we can offer our ears but not our hands, our feet but not our eyes. Your sex organ is part of your body and is to be sacrificed to God.

You've probably heard the joke about the pig and the chicken. The pig and the chicken are in the barn, and the chicken says, "We should give the farmer a ham-and-egg breakfast." "That's easy for you to say," said the pig. "For you it's just an offering, for me it's a total sacrifice."

I think it's a great idea to give our Lord and Savior—the One who became human, died, and rose from the dead—a complete sacrifice, including our sex organs. Paul concluded that this sacrifice is *a spiritual act of worship.*

I travel across the country speaking at conferences in different churches—Catholic, Presbyterian, Baptist, Methodist, Full Gospel, Four Square, non-denominational, interdenominational, community, and many others. I have been blessed to attend contemplative worship services as well as more demonstrative services.

Whether we sit, stand, clap, raise our hands, or sing out loud, it is not complete worship if God doesn't own all of us. When we are totally clean, God himself is Lord of our sexuality.

Let's make this practical, shall we? You might be thinking, *How do I ask God if it's okay for me to masturbate, look at pornography, engage in immorality, or commit adultery?* Some people feel that since they don't hear the audible voice of God speak when they ask God a question, they can to do whatever they want to instead of obeying the clear commandment from the Word of God.

When you are tempted, sometimes your mind isn't working right. So allow me to make this simple. The next time you're tempted to look at porn, masturbate, or act out in other sexual behaviors that do not include your wife, consider this: your pastor is a spiritual authority over you as a shepherd over his flock. The next time you're tempted to do anything sexually inappropriate, ask his permission. Since your sex organ does *not* belong to you, you don't get to make the decisions. You making a decision about your sex organ is like you going into a parking lot and stealing someone else's car and taking it for a drive. That car doesn't belong to you, and you don't have the authority or ownership to decide what to do with that car. It's not yours.

In the exact same way, your sex organ has been bought, meaning the deed to your sex organ doesn't have your name at the top but rather that of Jesus Christ, Lord of all. If you are under authority, then you have to ask permission. You are blessed if you are under authority, and let's say, *not blessed* if you are not under authority.

Here's how this works. You're sitting at your desk at your office. You have a little down time and you're thinking, *Maybe I can look at some bathing suit or lingerie ads, porn, or go somewhere to masturbate.* Sounds crazy, right? But it happens. Before you could push a button, *you'd have to call your pastor to ask permission:* "Pastor John, this is Bob Smith. I'm at work and I am thinking about looking at some porn and masturbating, but since my sex organ belongs to God, and you are his shepherd over me, I have to ask your permission. So what do you think? Can I?"

You can probably imagine Pastor John's long pause. Then you can imagine the questions he might ask and the verses he might quote—because his brain is working just fine at the moment. And then there is that amazing prayer he would pray over you and the encouragement he would give to you to become all you can be in Christ. And last, there's the "I'll see you Sunday."

Imagine if every man in the body of Christ followed this principle. Do you think there would be nearly as many men struggling with sexual sin and sexual addiction? Fewer, I guarantee you. Not only would men not act out or defile themselves as often, they would be inspired to stay clean. I am 100 percent committed to calling my pastor before I would consider doing anything sexually inappropriate, including looking at pornography. His cell number is in my phone, and I informed him that when he became my pastor, my sexuality was placed under his authority. I told him I would call before, not after, any sexually inappropriate behavior. Some men might feel embarrassed to actually do this. I, however, would be more embarrassed if I didn't have this friendship as a safety net. I always believe it's better to humble yourself even if it is embarrassing rather than be humiliated by a greater issue.

I am under authority because I have given the decision about my sexuality over to God through my pastor. Who decides for you? If it's you, you could be in real trouble because you don't own your sex organ.

Being under authority has given me more than two and a half decades of freedom, because I don't have to make the decision. An attorney reportedly said that he who defends himself has a fool for a client. I would say sexually it is showing wisdom to be under authority. You are blessed to be under authority.

When I share this at men's conferences I ask, "Who is the first owner of your sex organ?" In one large, masculine voice, they say "God!"

Owner #2

I know some of you are curious. I said there were three owners; the first is God, and as I pointed out you're actually the last owner of your sex organ. Who is number two?

Number two is the most amazing person you have ever

met or will ever meet. She is beautiful, godly, and way more than you could ever deserve. That's right! She is the woman you committed to or will commit to love, honor, and cherish when you said those incredible words while exiting your single life: "I do."

If you're married, remember the day you got dressed up whether you wanted to or not? You invited all your friends and family who could come to witness the death of your singleness and the resurrection of this new entity called marriage. You smiled, you ate, maybe you danced, and boy were you looking forward to being alone with her that night, right?

Let's back up a minute and go back to the altar. There is something astounding that occurred at your altar experience, something you may have missed in all the excitement and hormones. On that day, at that altar of marriage, a sex-organ title transfer occurred. That's right; your wife became the second official God-ordained owner of your sex organ.

She owns your sexuality! Don't believe me? Let's go to the Word of God. "For the wife does not rule over her own body but the husband does; likewise the husband does not rule over his own body, but the wife does" (1 Corinthians 7:4 RSV). Your body—and we already established your sex organ is part of your body—does not belong solely to you but to your wife. You might be unclear about this, but take a moment and ask your wife if she believes on that day she was to receive all of you, and if when you committed to forsake all others, that included forsaking yourself as well. You were to forsake everybody, and your sex organ was only for her. Give her a call and ask her.

Your wife owns your sexuality. She has authority over this area, and that is God's way of protecting and providing for you sexually. I tell guys attending my conference to go home and tell your wife she owns your sex organ. The reactions are amazing when you acknowledge her ownership.

Let's make this practical. Truth is valuable if you apply it in your own world. So you're back at the desk at work. You're having urges to view inappropriate images or pornography, or maybe you want to masturbate or flirt with a female coworker. If you are under authority, after you call Pastor John, you call your wife. Imagine that conversation. "Hon, this is your husband. I'm at work, got some downtime and I thought I would look and lust after other women, you know Victoria's Secret, then try some hardcore pornography and maybe even masturbate. Since you are the owner of my sex organ, I have to ask your permission since I am under your sexual authority." For single guys, use the second phone call for an accountability person.

Pastor John may have asked you some questions, but your wife is going to have a different set of questions. She may question your sanity, love, commitment to the family, why you would risk losing your job, and where you might sleep that evening or next week. She might pray for you, quote Scripture, and encourage you, especially since you're calling before you do anything, and you are honoring her first above yourself. And you're calling her to help you, not to destroy you. It just might be bumpy in the beginning.

Because you might have some apprehension about being under her sexual authority, you would have to make the call for permission, and not forgiveness, which is the motto of those under authority. Forgiveness not permission is the motto of those in rebellion against authority.

If men walked under sexual authority and called their wives *before* they acted inappropriately sexually, do you think there would be more or less sexual sin in the global body of Christ? Less—and I am absolutely sure of this. This submission to our two owners by itself could put sexual sin in remission in the church. Most men are not under sexual authority. Therefore they are not experiencing the blessings of being under authority. I am under such authority. I have made not a promise but a covenant, which to me means I will absolutely do this no matter what, no excuses not to call my wife if I even seriously think about inappropriate sexual behaviors. I am a blessed man because of this. I have never had to make that call, but I know one thing; if my brain wasn't working right and I seriously thought about acting out, regardless of the mood my pastor is in, my wife would be 100 percent sane and I could trust her judgment sexually, and so forgo being a disgrace to myself, my God, her, our family, and all those I have served in the past and will serve in the future.

Being under sexual authority is freeing. My sexual organ's decisions are not mine to make. They are God's through my pastor and my wife. Some of you may call yourself single and think this doesn't apply to you.

No person is single if he or she is a Christian. You are married to Christ. Your spiritual Facebook status is married without a spouse. *Single* denotes an idea of freedom that slaves of Christ do not have. You will most likely be married one day. Honor your future wife with your life. Filling yourself with porn and lust dishonors yourself, your God, and your future wife. Be clean and accountable as you wait for her. The discipline you develop in this stage is the same discipline you will need to be clean and faithful to your spouse when God brings her into your life.

Owner #3

Finally we get to talk about the third owner of your sex organ—you. Most of you probably started reading this chapter believing the world's lie that you are the CEO of your sex organ. All through these pages a small voice may have been crying out, "Mine, mine, mine!" like a child with his favorite toy.

The truth is your sex is not just yours—it's God's, your wife's, and *then* yours. You and I are not a CEO or other executive in this company; we are the janitors of this sexual corporation. We get bathroom duty only. If you are doing anything else as a married man, then you are out from under authority. Why do you think the devil can keep messing with you for years? If you are out from under authority, you are wearing a big target for the devil to aim at. And if you continue to feed your perverted lust, lust will grow for sure.

Once you start down a path of sexual independence and rebellion against your sexual authorities, there is no telling where that path will lead. As a janitor, however, you only get bathroom rights. That is the only authority I have sexually in my life, otherwise I have to use my cell phone to ask permission.

Americans like to vote. But the kingdom of God is a monarchy. He alone is King; we are only servants. Servants are told what to do. I tell young men all the time that if they don't like to be told what to do, heaven's going to be hell for them. I've settled the issue of being under authority. I hope this conversation helps you also accept that you are not the king or owner of your sex organ.

This freedom of making decisions about your sex organ and trusting others to make those decisions can help you enjoy the journey of the Christian life without guilt or shame. Let me put this principle into four simple words. Put them on your cell phone, screen saver, a Post-it note, any place where you can be reminded of them: *God, wife, me, pee.*

Yes, you can summarize sexual authority in those four words. God is the first owner. Your wife is the second owner. And you are the third owner, which gives peeing rights only. This revelation can help you get and stay clean. When you accept your place in this hierarchy, you will be free indeed.

After I share this truth at a conference, we take a ten- to fifteen-minute break. Many men's conferences occur on Saturday mornings. The men get their eggs, biscuits, bacon, and coffee. After a bit, the coffee needs to exit the body and I'll visit the men's room, where I've heard this joke many times: "Doc, I'm doing the only thing I'm allowed to do." We laugh, but accepting this as truth has brought freedom to many men.

My hope is that you will walk under the sexual authority God has placed over you so you can reach the spiritual authority he would like to give you. There is much more at stake here than sex—it is totally about the kingdom of God.

9

A Promised Land

We have all heard the many marvelous stories in which God gave his people the promised land. Sometimes we hear these stories so often that we begin to characterize them in a reduced form. As guys we are often guilty of not wanting too many details—we'd much rather get to the point. Our summarizing can limit our ability to appreciate a story's nuance.

I am guilty of wanting to summarize so that I can move on to the next point or to something I think is more important. More than fifteen years ago I had a saintly secretary in my office. She was an amazing worker, very organized and extremely personable. I only had a few minutes between clients, so I would need all my information on phone calls in that short window of time. I had to ask for the summary version, or one-sentence version, to avoid spending ten minutes on each call. The "Just-the-facts-ma'am" approach.

Some men summarize God giving the people of Israel the promised land so that it sounds something like this, "God gift-wrapped the land, so they walked in and now live in the promised land." Let's expand on this just a little. Yes, God performed many miracles for the people of Israel during the battles. You remember the miraculous crossing of the Jordan and the walls of Jericho falling down?

Originally, the inheritance of Israel, this promised land, was going to be a cooperation between the God of heaven and the Israelites' sweat and sacrifice. As Americans, we view inheritance as our parents or parent working really hard, saving a bunch of money, and bequeathing it to us upon their deaths. We did nothing for it—we inherit it.

God promised the people of Israel the promised land as their inheritance. God didn't just give it to them, however; they had to kill and be killed to inherit it. In multiple battles, there were many heroes and those who lost their lives to see this inheritance come to pass for those they loved.

I live in a military town with two air force bases, an army base, and an air force academy. I see these brave men and women everywhere: restaurants, malls, and churches. Some days the news reports the deaths of those who were stationed locally. They died for our freedom, and that is the greatest sacrifice of all—to give one's life for those one loves.

In the book of Joshua, we are introduced to such men.

These men had already received 100 percent of their inheritance from God. They already had their new home, and their wives and families were excited about all God had done. They had cows, goats, chickens, and had neighbors to tell stories to in the evening by the fire. After years in the desert eating manna, they were now cooking steaks on the grill. Life couldn't be any better for the two-and-a-half tribes that inherited the land on this side of the Jordan. However, there was a significant problem. Their brothers had not yet received their inheritance. Their brothers, not having all that God had for them, were their main concern. Let's go to Scripture and read this detailed part of the story of inheritance.

Here, God parts the Jordan just as he did the Red Sea, and the tribes cross over to do battle. This is what it says of those two-and-a-half tribes of men who had already received their inheritance: "The men of Reuben, Gad and the half-tribe of Manasseh crossed over, armed, in front of the Israelites, as Moses had directed them. About forty thousand armed for battle crossed over before the LORD to the plains of Jericho for war" (Joshua 4:12–13).

It is amazing that forty thousand men decided to leave luxury, their wives, their children, and their new land and home to go fight for a land that wasn't ever going to be theirs. They fought so their brethren could have a home and land. They fought for others' inheritance. To me, that is masculinity in its finest display.

You might be asking, *What does this story have to do with me, or—even better—what does this have to do with men living a clean life*? The answer is, a lot. In the Old Testament, the gift or inheritance of God was the promised land. This inheritance had to be fought for, and people had to die. It's not as though the Israelites showed up and said to all the local people, "God said this is ours. You have to move now," and the people moved. They fought the Israelites to the death to try to keep them from taking their homes and land.

This Old Testament inheritance is symbolic of the inheritance in the New Testament, which is not a portion of geographical land. Instead this gift from God is the very nature of Christ. He died not only to give us eternal life in the future but to give us his personality of love, purity, gentleness, and meekness here on earth. He died so we could become like him. Just as in the Old Testament, however, our flesh doesn't just walk out when Jesus walks into our lives. We have to kill our flesh to gain our inheritance of his nature. We have to kill our sinful nature and walk by the Spirit, as Paul admonished us:

> So I say, live by the Spirit, and you will not gratify the desires of the sinful nature. For the sinful nature desires what is contrary to the Spirit, and the Spirit what is contrary to the sinful nature. They are in conflict with each

other, so that you do not do what you want. But if you are led by the Spirit, you are not under the law.

The acts of the flesh are obvious: sexual immorality, impurity and debauchery; idolatry and witchcraft; hatred, discord, jealousy, fits of rage, selfish ambition, dissensions, factions and envy; drunkenness, orgies, and the like. I warn you, as I did before, that those who live like this will not inherit the kingdom of God.

But the fruit of the Spirit is love, joy, peace, patience, kindness, goodness, faithfulness, gentleness and self-control. Against such things there is no law. Those who belong to Christ Jesus have crucified the sinful nature with its passions and desires. Since we live by the Spirit, let us keep in step with the Spirit. (Galatians 5:16–25)

Definitely part of killing our flesh is walking in the Spirit, which is love. Love is the opposite of lust. Lust and love cannot exist at the same place at the same time. Lust and love are as polar opposite as light and darkness. You have to leave light to enter darkness. You have to leave darkness to enter light. In the same way, we have to leave love to lust and leave lust to love.

How do we leave lust? That is a great question! Let's address this and then I want to give you some tips to help you and your brothers inherit your land of freedom in Christ.

Paul addressed this issue when he told us to "Treat younger men as brothers, older women as mothers, and younger women as sisters, with absolute purity" (1 Timothy 5:1–2). Paul gives us some insight into leaving lust and entering love. Paul was telling Timothy that when it comes to women, and men for that matter, to always put them in a relationship context.

Let's take a moment to review, and contrast a relationship context to an object relationship with a woman. When you look at a woman lustfully, you are assessing her packaging. You're looking solely at physical features: faces and body parts. You have to reduce her to one-dimensional to be able to lust. Paul is telling us to put each woman, regardless of age, into a relational context. It is doubtful you will lust after your mom or your sisters. You see them as complete, three-dimensional people. You see them as mothers, sisters, believers, parents, and so on. You see them in a relational context.

When you look at a woman through your relational lens, you will have a much harder time lusting than if you don't. I realize some women dress as if they are merely objects, but that doesn't matter. Jesus, in Luke 7:37–38, had a sinful woman wiping and kissing his feet, but he didn't lust after her. He kept her in a lust-free context.

When you see a woman and you feel yourself sliding toward lust, you can put the brakes on by putting her in a relational context and praying for her.

For example, Joe is in his usual place at the local coffee shop. He is sitting there minding his own business, when in walks an attractive woman who appears to be a lost woman spiritually. He does fine as she walks by and places her order for a fat-free latte. He even hears the male barista flirt with her a little. Then she decides to sit right in front of Joe. He can see her just above his laptop.

Joe's inner boy and spiritual man are struggling. Joe's inner boy is saying, *She's hot. She wants to be looked at. What's a look, anyway? C'mon she may never be here again. C'mon Joe, look.* Joe's inner man is saying, *Don't look. You have had so much victory. Send an e-mail to Pastor John and get out of here before you do something you'll have to confess later. Remember, victory.*

The battle wages like this in almost all men at times. Here is a way to stay in a love position versus a lust position: pray for her. I don't mean get out of the chair and walk across the store, church, or to wherever she is and introduce yourself as Mr. Spiritual. I mean in your heart, your mind, or even if you have to, in another room, out loud. Joe has learned that when this battle hits, he can pray a single prayer like this one:

God, this woman was created by you. She is your favorite daughter. If she is not saved, then lead her to the Lord. I pray for her husband (present or future), her children, and her parents that they would all know you and be blessed by your salvation in Jesus' name.

A simple, heartfelt prayer takes this attractive woman and puts her in a relational context. She is no longer a hot object; she is God's daughter, a mother, a wife. Joe has put the brakes on lust and put the gas pedal on love. He still may need to move, get focused on something else, or leave, depending on his inner strength or connection to the Spirit at that time. But he *can* silence the inner boy and see the woman as a daughter of God.

Take a minute and experience how God might feel about us lusting after one of his daughters. Let me give you a little perspective. You're at a local restaurant that you and your wife frequent. You're eating a favorite meal, enjoying each other's company and laughing at things you might normally laugh at.

You start to notice there is a guy in the restaurant who keeps staring at your wife. You look over, and sure enough he is still looking at her. He's not looking at her as you would a person in the crowd; he is actually lusting after her, checking out her body, hoping you go to the restroom so he can slip her a card. He's not seeing your wife as a person or a mom, just a thing he is entitled to lust after.

How are you feeling toward this guy? Well, I don't imagine very positive. You might think he is a creep who has problems, but at the very least you're uncomfortable, and at worst protective or angry.

Let's take this example a little further. A week later you are at the same restaurant with your daughter. She's looking beautiful, and you're enjoying your time together, ordering your favorite appetizer and talking about her friends. You notice the same guy. This time he is staring and lusting after your little girl. You can tell he is looking at her inappropriately. His eyes are glazed over, as he keeps ogling your precious daughter.

Now how are you feeling? I'm thinking you cruised right by feeling uncomfortable and now you are angry. Who does this guy think he is to objectify one of the most amazing little girls in the world? You, or I, for that matter, would be ready to fight him if he came near her. We have no real positive thoughts towards this man, do we?

Take this example and apply it to you and God. He created this amazing daughter, whom he loves and celebrates, and there you are at the mall, restaurant, work, or on the Internet lusting after her. You're sexualizing her in some manner. At that moment, how do you think God feels toward you? I'm not sure how he feels, but I don't think it's real positive. At the very least, I guess he would be disappointed. After all, he died so we could be free. He filled us with his Spirit so we would love all women at all times. Since he is a man, he might get irritated, especially if this is the state of your heart on a regular basis.

God does have feelings, and he has feelings toward us men. I hope this helps to see that all women, regardless of what they believe about themselves, are favorite daughters of God.

Today, the men in the church are in the biggest battle in church history. This is the fight to stay clean. Yet, we have a significant flaw in our rules of engagement. You know the rules we use to actually fight our opponent. These rules tells us what we can and can't do. Those who have served in the military know what I mean by "rules of engagement." They were told by superiors they couldn't do this or that when engaging the enemy, limiting their ability to fight the enemy. The church for the most part has an unspoken rule of engagement that is crippling our side from winning. This limitation is best explained by a policy many churches have when it comes to sexual issues.

The church as a whole has a "don't ask, don't tell" policy of engagement with lust and sexual immorality. Simply put, this policy by the leadership and male culture of the church is that they are committed by "tradition" not to ask questions about your sexuality. If you go to church, there is almost an oath that you won't be asked directly about your sexuality. You won't be asked about whether or not you are looking at pornography. You will never be directly asked if you are masturbating. You will never be asked if you are flirting with women or having affairs.

This is the "don't ask" part of the policy of church leaders, pastors, and the general male church culture. In this tradition, the cancer of sexual sin, pain, and suffering of men has grown exponentially in the last few decades.

The other part of this tradition, "don't tell," is held up by the rank and file of men in the church. If you're lusting, viewing porn, masturbating, flirting, cheating, or anything inappropriate, don't tell. Don't tell yourself, your wife, and your spiritual leaders. Keep your sexual behaviors a secret. We all know this is unbiblical, and I'll address this more in future chapters, but most of us know this is how the church male culture is currently operating.

Most churches have this same policy for singles in the church as well. In a nutshell, the policy goes like this, "We won't ask you singles about pornography use, masturbation, or premarital sex with each other, and you don't tell us and everyone just pretends we are all okay."

We have to look at both sides of this ineffective policy if we are going to make any sort of change. Both parts of this policy are very comfortable to our flesh. It's very easy to pretend every guy you know in church is lust-free, and that they don't go to adult bookstores or websites or cheat on their wives. When you live in this type of world, it's great. There is no need to ask or tell, because everyone is just fine.

I remember, early in my career, talking to a pastor about speaking to his men on sexual addiction. He said frankly, "We don't have that problem in our church." Today most pastors are not that naïve. The Internet has forced pastors and the church at large to face this cancerous enemy. However, traditions have not changed.

Take a moment and count how many years you have been a Christian. For many of you it's been several, and for others like me, it's been decades. You most likely have heard sermons or other teachings, one-way monologues on sexual purity of some kind, but has a man asked you straight up about porn, masturbation, lust, or sex outside of marriage? Seriously think how many times a man from the church has left the comfort of his world to invade yours and asked, "So, Lou, have you looked at porn lately?"

How many times has it been? One, two, five, or more? Or are you in the same boat as most American men who have never been asked straight up about this? You read earlier about statistics that point to a major war involving men in sexual trouble of all kinds. How is it that so many of us still act as though there is no war? We simply do what's comfortable for us.

I suggest we change this policy of don't ask, don't tell and instead unleash our army with new standards of engaging this battle. I suggest we go to an *ask* policy. This means that, like the two-and-a-half tribes who crossed the Jordan, we leave our comfort zones of "I have mine." Many of your brothers in your local church don't have the full inheritance Christ died to give them. They are trapped in a secret world and most of Christ's brave warriors do not have the testosterone to ask some simple questions on a regular basis.

How do I know? Because I have traveled to churches of almost every denomination, giving men these hero tools to invade their brothers' entrapment. Many have told me they are free from that point forward because a man looked them straight in the eye and asked them the questions straight up.

Asking the Questions

Here's how it works. Cameron, your friend whom you have known for years, goes to the same church as you. You have been to men's events and served together here and there. You have seen Cameron's sons grow up to be teenagers, and you like his wife.

It's your average Sunday, and you're standing around the foyer in front of the church with people walking about. You see Cameron as you do most Sundays. You catch his eye and move forward for your handshake. Make sure he is alone, not with his family or friends. You grab his right hand to shake it, and with your left hand on his wrist you look him straight in the eye and ask some version of, "When was the last time you looked at porn?" or "When was the last time you masturbated?"

Keep your eyes looking directly at him and be aware of the grip strength in his right hand. Also notice if Cameron's eyes look off or down. Remember, you know Cameron, so you'll be aware if he is nervous. He might try to laugh you off, but stay focused. "No, seriously, when was the last time?" If Cameron is not struggling, he might say years or decades ago. If he is struggling, you are probably the first man who has loved him enough to help him claim his full inheritance from Christ. He might say a week or month ago or even this week. If he does get honest with you, do two things.

First, reassure him that the reason you asked was that you care and you want him to have all Christ has for him without any of the shame the enemy wants to give him. Second, tell him that you will walk with him through this as long as it takes. If the setting is appropriate, you can pray for Cameron so he knows you're really in this battle with him. Then let him know that you two should call or text daily to beat this together.

When you change the rules of engagement, you get different results. Many men are trapped simply because of the lifeless tradition of "don't ask, don't tell." We need to transform our Christian male culture into an ask-and-tell culture. If we change these ancient rules, we can have the most sexually pure men in our society. That could mean that as the culture gets sicker, our Christian men could lead in business, politics, science, and anywhere else life takes them.

This is the generation to break the rules and start asking the questions. I'll never forget a man I'll call Tom. I shared with him much of what you have read so far in this chapter. He heard that 50 percent of his brothers in his church were trapped. At my conference he experienced freedom in his prayer group of five people as they got honest with each other after being directly asked about porn and masturbation. Tom was so touched by his friends' openness that he began a personal crusade.

Tom was well liked by everybody. He was the head greeter at church and had the biggest smile every Sunday in the foyer. After I left the conference, Tom made it his personal mission to ask every man at the church who wasn't at the men's conference about their last time viewing porn and masturbating. Tom helped many men get honest. He also funneled many into the Freedom support groups the church had established for men who struggle with sexual addiction issues. One man changed the lives of many families in his local church.

Tom believed he was given a key to free men from their sexual prisons. He saw this as a tool to start a healing process. Tom himself hadn't struggled for many years with this issue, but he wasn't satisfied with only him and his family being free from lust and porn. He wanted that freedom for everybody. He wanted his brothers free. He wanted marriages not to be destroyed by secret sexual sin. He wanted men to live clean lives, not to just pretend when they came to church.

Every church needs a Tom, a man who cares enough to consistently break the don't ask, don't tell policy until it becomes the male culture of the church to ask and tell.

Not everyone will be honest. Even in those cases when the unconfessing men in Tom's church get caught or convicted, whichever comes first, you can bet they will come and talk to Tom because he is not afraid to engage on this issue.

I can't tell you how many elders, deacons, pastors, professionals, media ministers at all levels stop and talk to me about these things, simply because they know they can. Jesus needs sexual shepherds looking over the men in every congregation. You might think the concept of a sexual shepherd odd, but it's valuable. Often the sexual shepherd is *not* the senior pastor, although it could be. Look at this idea in other areas of your congregation.

You have a shepherd for the teenagers in your church, sometimes a paid staff person and sometimes a volunteer. You probably have a financial person who helps people with debts and budgets. A sexual shepherd is not an official title unless you're a men's minister, then you could easily get away with being this guy. You could easily say, "It's my job to ask." Sexually clean men make better husbands. They are less likely to commit adultery if they are being honest with another man. They are more likely to be better dads, friends, neighbors, and overall just better men. This is men's ministry at its essence.

I really hope some of you become like Tom. You may become the underground go-to guy whom the pastor sends men to, and you will be a hero to many. Over the years I have had many Toms determine that porn wasn't going to have a stronghold on their church—not on their shift. One man can make a significant difference in the lives of other men that impacts his church, his local community, and way beyond.

I hope you are encouraged by the promised land of Christ's nature, which he died to give you. For some of you, your flesh or sinful nature needs to be killed in order to walk free from the chains that may have held you. You can be victorious. You can also lead men to victory one at a time. You decide what policy of engagement you want to follow in your life and in your church.

James and John

I love Truth. I really mean I love him. Jesus is awesome, and he himself is truth. We often reduce truth to a fact or principle, but truth is a person. As we love and get to know truth, he reveals all kinds of things to us.

Most of us think Jesus limits himself just to biblical truth, creating, and wisdom, but I believe he reveals all kinds of things to men and women. He is the author of medical, scientific, and technical truths. The devil doesn't want any area of your life to improve, but Jesus desires for all your life to prosper.

Jesus wants every man reading these pages to not only become sexually clean but stay sexually clean and have an awesome sex life with the bride he has given him or will give him. Can you say amen to a God who wants all the very best for us?

I want you to know the heart of our God. He is 100 percent for you. He loves you as a person, a man, and as his favored son. He desires every binding chain, be it sexual or nonsexual, to be totally broken from your life. If our Father's desire is for our total freedom, why are so many men not tapping into this freedom? I have the answer, and for me it has been years in the discovery. When this answer is regularly applied you can have a life of being clean.

Like some of you reading these pages, I was as saved as I could be, yet still trapped. I was in Bible school and yet still fully sexually addicted to masturbation and pornography. I tried, cried, fasted, prayed, and memorized Scripture, but still I would fail again and again because I didn't understand a simple truth.

I was applying something I had learned and memorized from 1 John, but without understanding. Through years of counseling men, I realized I wasn't the only one who had memorized this Scripture and unsuccessfully tried to apply it. I realize now that I was totally uninformed of another biblical truth, and honestly, although somewhat ineffective, it was helping me feel a little better. I felt better because I was trying at least something to address my problem.

Here is the scripture: "If we confess our sins, he is faithful and just and will forgive us of our sins and purify us from all unrighteousness" (1 John 1:9).

I was confessing up a storm. I went to Jesus, sometimes more than once a day, confessing my lust and sexual sin, and you know what happened every time? He forgave me. I know I was forgiven. Many times I could feel and experience his forgiveness. I know I felt forgiveness and his cleansing me of that particular impurity.

I believe in the blood of Jesus. His blood is greater than any sin, be it sexual sin or some other. His blood is not only greater than my sins, my family's, city's, or nation's sins, but his blood is more powerful than all the nations of all time—past, present, and future. That's how powerful his blood is.

I am astonished by how many Christians honestly have more faith in their sin, than in Jesus' blood to forgive the sin. I see people repeatedly trapped in thinking and believing that their sin is somehow so special it nullifies the power of his blood. If you are trapped into believing your sin is that special, let me tell you, it's not! Your sin is not special or powerful. His blood paid the full price for any and all sins whether they are sexual sins or not. I strongly encourage men to believe in the blood, not in their sin.

There I was, week after week for years, going to Jesus, asking for forgiveness, and being forgiven but still misbehaving, and feeling not only trapped but also like a total failure. Some of you know exactly what I was feeling. I was starting to believe God didn't care or that I was terminally bad, broken, or simply a kingdom failure. This cycle of sinning, going to Jesus, feeling better, sinning, confessing to Jesus, feeling better, and sinning was really getting old.

I went to seminary and the cycle was further apart, but still present. Then God revealed to me the truth I was missing in order to get and stay clean and free, as I have for the last twenty-five years.

Before I give you that truth, let me take you on my journey to receiving it. I wish it were as simple as me reading it, believing it, and doing it, as you will have the opportunity to do. But God, for whatever reason, took me on a bit of a journey before I received the revelation that transformed my life. You already heard the first step of my journey of years of crying, trying, repenting, being forgiven. To put these years into perspective, the words *sex addict* had not even been coined, and the church wasn't talking about sex. This was in the early 1980s, before personal computers were common.

At this time, I was in seminary and my roommate had one of the first personal computers, but this was still way before the Internet. I was in a cycle of asking for forgiveness, and as clear as I have ever heard or been prompted by the Holy Spirit, I was being told to tell my roommate I masturbated. My first response was not, "Yes, Lord." It was more like, "Are you crazy? Tell someone, especially someone I see several times a day?" Honestly, I was flabbergasted, but I knew that I knew God was telling me to do this.

My roommate and I had a good relationship at this point.

We would pray together, have all kinds of theological conversations, and yes, talk about life and girls. This, however, was going to be a whole new level of conversation. I made a deal with God when I got saved that I would do whatever he asked. I thought this was the craziest thing God had asked me to do yet. I went to my roommate, told him about my struggles, and how God was telling me to tell him if I chose to do these behaviors. This was at least a decade before men were talking about accountability or accountability partners.

Then it happened. I acted out by masturbating and then realized to be obedient I would have to tell my roommate. So I did—I told him. He was gracious, forgave me, and prayed for me. I never in my life felt so small and humbled. Then it happened again, a couple of weeks later, and again I confessed and felt small and humble, but this time something happened. I started to get free. I knew if I acted out I would have to tell, and I didn't want to keep admitting my poor choices, so I stopped for quite a while. When I married, I transferred this accountability to my wife and another male accountability partner, and now I have been free for more than a quarter of a century.

What happened was miraculous. I was getting clean and free, but why? I was still praying, reading, going to church, but why was I getting victory? I was simply applying a different principle. Later, and I mean much later, God showed me this principle in his Word: "Therefore confess your sins to each other and pray for each other so that you may be healed. The prayer of a righteous man is powerful and effective" (James 5:16).

I look at this Scripture now, and it is really obvious to me that I was missing a big piece of the puzzle. I find it interesting that James assumes we are all going to sin. I'm amazed at how many Christians forget after a while that they still sin regularly, even daily. I'm a sinner who was saved and I am still sinning—I hope less each year, but I still sin.

James is clear on what to do with sin: confess it to each other. Notice James wasn't highlighting confessing it to Jesus; he focused on confessing it to each other. Also notice James isn't making this optional but commands us to confess to each other when we sin "so that [we] may be healed." When we humble ourselves, as I did to my room-mate, and acknowledge our sin, even the sexual sins, we can be healed!

That's what is so exciting. It's not just sexual sin; it can be greed, gluttony, anger, over-entertaining (too much tele-vision or the like), or any other of the multitude of sins. It is really good news that there is a way not only to be forgiven but also to be healed.

There is a big difference between forgiveness and heal-ing. This difference is why so many Christian men today are stuck. They are not confessing to each other; they are only confessing to Jesus. When you confess to Jesus, you get forgiven. When you confess to another Christian man, you get healed. Most men are forgiven. They are not healed of sexual sin because they are not doing what God's Word commands, and that is confessing to their brother.

Some of you are thinking, *I'll just tell my wife.* It's great to tell your wife, but she is not a man, and you are putting her in a place she isn't designed for. She may not understand, and you know she won't ask you the same questions that a man would. Confessing to another man takes real testosterone, and you and I both know that, so don't take a shortcut. Men make men.

It's interesting to me that James puts the responsibility of confessing on the person who sins. It's not your pastor's job, your wife's job, or even your accountability partner's job to dig it out of you. You, as a man, are to bring it forth and confess it openly to your brothers. When you keep it to yourself, it is flat-out disobedience. Remember another Scripture: "Anyone, then, who knows the good he ought to do and doesn't do it, sins" (James 4:17). It's flat-out disobedience if you sin sexually and don't confess it to another man. That's why so many men are stuck.

Why do they stay stuck? Because of pride, plain and simple. We don't want anyone thinking less of us, so we keep our secrets to ourselves. This pride is a guarantee to stay sick. Let's take James 5:16 and put everything in reverse for a minute. In reverse this Scripture might read, "Don't confess your sin to each other so that you are guaranteed to stay sick and your prayers won't go far." That would stink, right? I can tell you, this is the plan of most men in the church regarding their sexual sins. They don't confess, they don't get better, and they wonder why they are not growing spiritually.

Outside of maybe praying with guys during the altar call, when was the last time you had a Christian brother come up to you and say, "John, I need to tell you I lusted, looked at porn, masturbated to lustful images, flirted outside of my marriage, cheated on my wife, or went to an adult bookstore"? For most of us this has never occurred, and yet at least half of the men are sexually sinning regularly in the church. You can be absolutely forgiven by Jesus, and absolutely not healed, if you and I are not confessing our sexual sins to each other.

Now I don't believe James means we need to confess to every man, just one other man. The guys who are in Freedom groups—Christian sex-addiction recovery groups of some kind—practice these principles regularly and are probably some of the cleanest and most honest men sexually in the church.

If you're not in such a group, you can find a man you trust to keep your confidence. There are many men in any church with whom you could be honest if you needed to. I'm strongly suggesting you need to, if you ever hope to be clean. I would even go so far as to say, if you are not willing to humble yourself to another man regularly, you will not get clean. You will try again, and again, by yourself, through sheer willpower, to stop again, but you will fail again, and stop again, and fail again. If that has been your pattern for years or decades, stop the pride. That's why you are not getting healed. To heal and get clean from sexual sin for your entire life, you must confess to another man.

If you are unwilling to do this ongoing confession, and not just one time at a men's conference, you will continue to be saved but sexually sick. You do run the risk of your behavior going further than you currently believe you will go. You run the risk of hurting your wife, future wife, children, or parents when this behavior comes to light.

There are two paths to humility. The first is the easiest path, and that is to humble yourself. You take the initiative to be honest and authentic. I have found for myself and thousands of other men that this is not only the easiest path, its consequences are small in comparison to the second option. The second option is you refuse to humble yourself. God will try to get you to get honest many times, but you'll refuse. You protect your sin from getting true healing, and it grows in your life. Then, *whamo*, it happens; you get exposed publicly in some manner.

I have been an eyewitness to many men who thought they would never get caught. God loves you too much to let your secrets kill you, so exposing them is an act of his grace and mercy. On the receiving side of this grace, however, it feels like total humiliation. Now several people know about that secret sexual sin. The consequences to this path of humility, called *humiliation*, can be staggering. I have seen men lose their wives, children, businesses, or ministries because they chose not to confess their sins to another person.

Humiliation hurts to the core. I could fill quite a huge container with the tears from the families of men who made their own plans to get better sexually. The plan of pride hurts a lot. That is why James told us to confess to each other, so we can avoid humiliation and just deal with a little sting from humbling ourselves.

What kind of man do you confess to? Let me give you a few options. First, any man who is deemed spiritually mature, who won't repeat your sins to another, would be a great person for your confession. If a man has a personal testimony of victory in this area, he would be a great person to confess to. A spiritual authority or spiritual leader can also be a helpful man here. These people might be pastors, elders, deacons, Sunday school teachers, or fill other positions in your local church. Christian counselors can be helpful. If they are licensed by the state, they cannot legally tell anyone about your sexual sin unless that sin involves sexual behavior with a minor, which they are legally obligated to report.

I have a great team of counselors who work alongside me. A telephone session with a professional counselor can be a confidential way to get started confessing your sexual sins, so you can have a point to begin applying this principle in your life.

Head and Body

John was telling us that going to Jesus for forgiveness is great for forgiveness, and he is advising us to go to our brothers for healing. This is awesome for those of us who want to walk clean for our entire lives. But why the "separation of powers"?

That is a question I wrestled with as well. Why couldn't I just do it all with Jesus? I prefer the least painful route. My question went deeper than my own shallowness. Over time I have come up with a theology that has helped me solve this dilemma.

Let's suppose you're going to a Costco or Sam's Club. Your local mega store is set up with all the groceries in the middle. On one side of the building is the area where you buy new tires and have them mounted. On the other side of the same store is the place where they change the oil in your car. Both the tire department and the oil department are part of the same company. The same company pays the employees of the oil department and the tire department.

It's Saturday at 7:00 a.m. and you want to get your tires changed before the family gets out of bed. You are unshowered and dressed in sweatpants and a baseball cap to cover up your bedhead. On the way you stopped for coffee because you're going to have to wait a while. Because you're not fully awake, you pull your car into the left side of the store and you walk up to the guy at the counter and you start explaining the type of tires you want and ask if they have them in stock and if they are on sale. He patiently listens to you while two other guys start walking into the store dressed as you are. At the end of your monologue you are surprised to hear the clerk tell you, "Sir, I would like to help you, but this is the oil department, not the tire department." You might huff, or sigh, or if you're in a bad mood, argue with him about why he won't change your tires. The reality is, you went to the wrong department for what you needed.

Jesus is the head of the body of Christ. You can read Ephesians 1:22 and 5:23, and Colossians 2:19 to see that the role of the head is to hold the body together. He is the firstborn, preeminent Son of God and the head of his church. Then there are all the Scriptures about the body of Christ (Romans 12:4; 1 Corinthians 12:12–27; and Ephesians 4:16). These Scriptures highlight that we are an amazing unit of God's body. We all have gifts and functions in this amazing body; and for the body to be healthy, we are to love one another and be about our particular functions.

The healing ministry of Christ is a body ministry the majority of the time. Before his crucifixion and resurrection, Jesus was healing people all the time. The postresurrection Jesus was with the few on the road to Emmaus, and then with the disciples for more than forty days (Acts 1:3)—and there is no record of anyone getting healed. Then, after the ascension and Pentecost, you see healing happening through the apostles repeatedly.

The healing ministry of Jesus is in the church, the body of Christ. He could do it all by himself, but the majority of the time he allows healing to flow through the body, and in regards to our discussion, it comes through our ongoing confession to our brothers.

Reasons We Don't Confess

Following are some observations from more than twenty-five years of listening to men who have had repeated opportunities to confess before they became humiliated. As we've discussed, the first reason why men don't confess about their porn, masturbation, flirting, or sex acts outside of marriage is pride.

We are too proud to admit that we are actively participating in a secret sin. We don't want to humble ourselves to our spouses, pastors, or brothers because we are proud. We all know that pride is not good and God will eventually deal with all of us who have pride. Let me warn you that it is so much more painful to make God spank us than it is to humble our pride and talk to a brother who is most likely going to be kind to us. Take a second and think how you would respond to a friend who confided to you that he is struggling. You would be kind because you know how much testosterone it took to confess to you.

But there are many more reasons men don't confess to their brothers. The second reason is hard to believe: men don't want to change. They actually believe they can continue to sow lust and sin and not reap any consequence. They love their sin. All of us have been in a season where we loved our sin prior to either repenting or having consequences.

That is the third reason: loving our sin. What you love, you protect. If you are protecting your secret sin, then that is what you love. It's possible to love porn, masturbation, online chatting, and sex outside of marriage more than we love God, ourselves, our spouses, our children, our future, and our future generations.

I'm a recovering sex addict and have worked with men on the entire continuum of struggling—from a little bit to massively, wholeheartedly addicted. We must believe our behaviors, not our theories, theologies, or philosophies.

If you are confessing to a brother, then you want a clean life. It is the only way to stay clean that truly works. If you were not confessing to a brother before reading this chapter, you could claim ignorance of this truth, but you now know that to be clean and stay clean you need to continually confess your faults one to another.

If you say that you deserve the forgiveness that Jesus supplies and you also deserve the healing from the body of Christ by confessing to another brother, then I believe you. Find a man you can talk to today, so that deep inside you can feel clean!

The Road to Trouble

The road to trouble is well traveled and well known. Millions of men in every culture have traveled it for thousands of years. Solomon wrote of a young man's road to trouble in Proverbs 7. The young man "finds" a woman and is seduced by his lust and her skills.

Here is the most important thing every man who travels this road to trouble has in common, in my varied experience. Not one of them realizes that he is on this road until he has traveled it for quite a while. There are distinct signs on this road, including Beware of Falling Rocks, Fire Danger, and an abundance of stop signs. Still, most men believe these signs are there for other men on this road, not for themselves. Most men think they know what they are doing and believe *they* won't let this road take them to the ultimate destination of adultery—or fornication, for our single brothers.

Let's look at the road Dewayne went down. At seventeen years of age, Dewayne accepted Christ as his Lord and Savior at a high school church event. Before coming to Christ, he was navigating his parents' divorce and had a lot of hatred for his stepmother, a woman his dad met and cheated with at a Chamber of Commerce meeting. Dewayne was really angry at his dad, but he couldn't show it because his dad was making his car payment and giving him money for almost anything he wanted.

Dewayne stayed with his dad because his dad kept the house, and Dewayne didn't want to live in an apartment with his mother and two sisters. Before meeting Christ, Dewayne was already deep into pornography and masturbating three to five times a week. He had five girlfriends during his high school years with whom he had sex. He cheated on two of them.

Dewayne's conversion was real. He started to go to church and tried to read his Bible. He still maintained his secret about pornography and masturbation. As he dated throughout college, he liked the Christian girls but often had a girl on the side who would have "just sex" with him. He met Susan a year after graduating from college. Susan was a Christian girl who had grown up in a stricter Christian faith than Dewayne. Dewayne respected her stance on sexual purity. She was beautiful, godly, had a good job, a nice car, and friends from her church. Dewayne kept his sexual stuff a secret from Susan and pretended he had more character than the way he was actually living when they married.

Life went on for Dewayne and Susan—that is until Dewayne was forty-five. They had three children along the way; one had just started college and the other two were in high school. Susan didn't work after the children were born. According to Dewayne, she always wanted things bigger and better, like their five-thousand-square-foot house and her Lexus. Dewayne became frustrated over the years because Susan didn't take care of the house, her car, or even herself.

Susan and Dewayne's relationship became more functional than relational. They attended church but other than that didn't spend any spiritual time together. Dewayne got better at golf; Susan got better at shopping, taking care of their children, hanging out with her girlfriends, and spending time with her miniature poodle, Mocha.

Dewayne was feeling more alone in the relationship. Susan was willing to only have sex in one position, and sex became less and less frequent. Dewayne was climbing the ladder at work, and with two more children going to college within the next few years, he felt obligated to work hard for the money to pay for everything. At work Dewayne was respected. He had been with the same company for almost twenty years. He was creative, ambitious, and believed in his team. He had won many industry awards that were scattered throughout his spacious office.

Dewayne had never read his Bible on any kind of regular basis. He went to church but was not involved in anything further. He was frequently on the Internet viewing pornography. He chatted sexually with a few women online but never followed through, and wasn't honest about his secret sexual outlet with anyone.

A new woman became a member of Dewayne's team at work. Carol was twenty-seven years old and was an eager worker. She was excited to have a job that was different from the waitressing and retail jobs she had held in the past. Carol was married but unhappy. Her husband worked deadbeat jobs and always made excuses for why he couldn't make it in the world. He went out with friends, drank some, and smoked pot on the weekends. They had a two-year-old child, but Carol felt as though she was the only parent.

Carol admired Dewayne and how successful and stable he seemed. Dewayne had only a little contact with Carol for her first few months on the job. When he did interact with her, however, he felt respected by her.

Dewayne and Carol interacted here and there, and Dewayne decided to give Carol a project at work. Carol thanked him profusely, and again looked at him respectfully. Dewayne liked the way he felt when he was around Carol. She brought out the good side of him.

As Dewayne and Carol continued to interact over the months, she shared her frustration of feeling like a single mom because of her husband's immaturity and irresponsibility. Dewayne began to share his frustration with his wife's ungratefulness and that she was not being very much fun. Over time, Dewayne and Carol began to bond and build a mutual respect for each other.

Dewayne began to fantasize about a relationship with Carol. She was respectful, took care of herself, was punctual, hardworking, and open-minded about things. He even began to fantasize about sex with her and started regularly masturbating to those fantasies. Carol also began to fantasize about how nice it would be to be taken care of, to be given jewelry, and not have to be a single parent. She was attracted to Dewayne's stability and his work ethic. She thought he was a really great guy.

Dewayne felt Carol's admiration grow and began to share more time with her. He gave her a rightfully deserved raise and in her excitement she gave him a hug and a kiss on the cheek. Dewayne was blown away and aroused by this. He couldn't stop thinking about Carol that whole day and night and the entire weekend.

Carol had a friend from college named Casey who was an attorney. The two of them did yoga together twice a week. That weekend Carol was embarrassed and told Casey what had happened. They agreed she should probably apologize to Dewayne. Carol didn't, however, tell her husband. She also couldn't stop thinking about Dewayne because he really believed in her and praised her, and she felt great around him.

Carol stuck to her plan and went to Dewayne's office on Monday to apologize. "There's my best worker," Dewayne said to Carol as she walked in.

"Thanks," she said more sheepishly than normal. Dewayne asked what was on her mind. Susan replied, "About Friday, I really appreciated the raise and bonus, and I got so excited, but I felt my hugging and kissing you on the cheek was inappropriate."

Dewayne smiled and said, "I think that's the best kiss I've had in years. No problem." They looked at each other, and both realized they liked each other in a more romantic way. They continued to work together. Then Dewayne had a project that required some travel to Florida. He chose Carol to go along for the experience.

On the trip they discussed their feelings for each other, and during that three days they went from holding hands, to hugs, to kisses, and a couple of sexual encounters. They agreed to keep it professional at work, but they both really "loved" each other.

Dewayne and Carol met for dinners and sex and traveled some more together. They didn't know where their relationship was going, but they were both enjoying themselves. Dewayne felt respected and loved Carol's gratefulness for even small gifts, and the sex was uninhibited. Carol couldn't believe that a successful man like Dewayne would love her. She felt he'd be a great dad if they married and she was still young enough to have more children. The flood of texting and contact grew steadily during the following eight months as their affair continued.

Then it happened. In Dewayne's case it was something he never could have imagined. Carol texted him, as she had many times before, to connect at a hotel for their rendezvous. This time when Dewayne came to the door, a tearstained Carol met him. Crying, she immediately hugged him and said, "I'm sorry, I'm sorry." Dewayne was clueless, but held her until she stopped crying. "I'm positive," she said. Dewayne didn't understand. She pulled an item out of her pocket and said, "I'm pregnant."

The blood immediately left Dewayne's face, and his hug became limp, although he still tried to be comforting. "What does this mean?" he blurted out.

"It's yours. I haven't had sex with my husband in two months, and it's definitely your baby." They lay together silently. Dewayne assured her he would want her to have the baby; he just needed a little time to figure it out, and asked for a couple of weeks to get his head on straight, and for her to do the same.

One week later Dewayne was you know where—in my office. Dewayne never thought he would be on this road to trouble and never thought he would be making decisions about ending two marriages, aborting or having a baby, or destroying his children's lives and breaking his wife's heart.

The road to trouble is a well-known road traveled by many men, even men who are Christians. Most of the men I have counseled in the last two decades, who have walked their road to trouble, are Christians. I want to highlight several principles to help you avoid getting on or traveling any farther on the road to trouble.

Adultery and fornication are real, and according to Scripture have many consequences for you and your family. Sex can destroy your future in so many ways. I have seen families, careers, ministries, and fortunes destroyed by men who traveled this road to trouble, never believing there would be a toll to pay for being on it. In the next several pages I want to give you some solid principles that can keep you from getting on the road to trouble, or provide an exit if you are already on it.

Principles to Keep You Off the Road to Trouble

1. Fear God

God is love, and he is to be ultimately respected for creating you and giving you blessings. It is God who is to be feared. When we fear God, we hate evil (Proverbs 8:13). Hating evil is a result of fearing God. It's much like your teenage years, when there were certain things you knew not to do because you knew your dad's stance on them, and you knew he would implement consequences.

Today in our churches we don't hear much about fearing God and respecting him. In fact, I can't think of the last time I heard a sermon on fearing God. I highly recommend you do a word study on the fear of the Lord at some point. There are so many benefits of a heart that fears God. One of the results is that you run from evil and do not entertain it or be entertained by it.

2. Be Honest

Dewayne was never honest with anyone about his secret sexual life until he came to my office. He was fifty years old before he disclosed his cheating on girlfriends, pornography, and masturbation. Being honest about your sexual past can bring healing. When you review your sexual past, you also learn cycles that can help you to break destructive patterns.

Dewayne had always had both a "good" girl and sexual girl or fantasy girl. Had Dewayne known about this pattern and stopped the porn and fantasy girl, then it's possible he could have been more satisfied in his marriage because he would not have compared his wife unfairly to others or remained glued sexually to twenty-year-old bodies as a fifty-year-old Christian man.

Dewayne's dishonesty about his past prevented him from healing and put him in a position to duplicate his past with Carol. Dewayne was also not honest about his present. He was not honest about his present pornography usage or flirting with women online. This set him up to justify inappropriate relationships and conversations with women. He also was not honest about the feelings and the positive charge he received from talking to women online.

Dewayne was not honest about how he was feeling toward his wife. He was ungrateful for the godly woman he had as a spouse. He focused on what he saw as her weaknesses. He wasn't honest with another man about these feelings. Had he talked to another guy, he could have received support and encouragement to work on himself and his attitude, or go to counseling.

Being honest is important if you want to avoid traveling on the road to trouble. Honesty can get you off this highway—or keep you from getting on this highway to begin with.

3. Talk to Your Wife

The women God gives us to be our wives are amazing. In most cases they are firmly on our sides. They want their marriages and families to last a lifetime. They married us looking for the happily ever after.

In most cases, women respond well to truth, especially early-on truth. If you have a secret porn life, it will be painful for her, but not nearly as painful as finding out about your involvement with another woman or other behaviors involving other people.

No marriage is perfect. Talking to your wife about issues in your marriage is healthy, and a sign you want the marriage to work. If you run into issues bigger than the two of you can handle, seek out a mentor couple, a pastor, or a Christian counselor. Often the presence of another person can help clarify the issues, and more minds are available to create solutions. Having others involved can add an element of accountability that "all by yourself" can't offer, and it can positively change the dynamics.

4. Don't Believe in a Secret

I am absolutely flabbergasted at how many men believe in secrets. They think that when encased in a secret, the truth will not be exposed. This is like the dog that puts his head under his paws thinking that because he can't see us, we can't see him. Jesus taught that what we do in secret will be shouted from the rooftops (Luke 12:2–3).

Revelation 2:23 teaches us that God knows our hearts, thoughts, and deeds. Hebrews 12:1 states we are surrounded by a cloud of witnesses. There is no such thing as a secret—period. You may have a season of lust and sin, but like a seed in the dirt, it will pop up.

Some guys think they are brighter than their wives or others. But no man is brighter than God. If you refuse to be honest, he can create circumstances that force the truth to be exposed. Trust me, I have seen his handiwork. I have heard of wives dreaming about exactly what their husbands were doing, children finding their dad's porn site or e-mails to girlfriends, and the other woman repenting and seeking forgiveness from the wronged wife.

I could go on for hundreds of pages with stories about how husbands who believed in secrets got caught. Sometimes they were big businessmen with hundreds of millions of dollars, pro-sports figures, top ministry leaders, politicians, doctors, lawyers, you name it—men at the top of their fields who believed in secrets.

I have taught my children to believe that you will be caught at every secret and every lie. Believing you will get caught is a better and healthier way to live and would keep every man off the road to trouble whether fornication or adultery.

5. Imagine the Worst

Imagining the worst is helpful, especially for the guys who dabble with fantasy, pornography, and masturbation who think they will never cross the line. Just suppose you did fornicate or commit adultery. First, list all the people it would affect if they found out. This list should include past, present, and future. People you grew up with; friends; family members; children; grandchildren; coworkers past, present, and future; neighbors; pastors; church members; people you ministered to; and so on. This list can easily number a hundred people, especially when each of them will be telling their friends and hairdressers. If you didn't already list them, add Jesus and God to the list.

Then take each person and imagine two things. First, imagine how they would feel the moment they heard the news of your falling. They might feel sad, mad, disappointed, betrayed, defrauded, conned, insignificant, and unimportant. Second, write down the consequences you might experience because of your behavior. Your consequences may be financial because your business was affected, the inability to go to college, loss of respect from your son, STDs, or unwanted pregnancies.

That's the power of one man's decision. It's helpful to see the mega impact your decision can have. Knowing the impact of you falling helps you desire to protect those close to you from that pain and stay away from the road to trouble.

6. Exit and Entrance Signs

Every public building you walk into has exit signs over the doors. Many buildings will also have entrance signs on the door they want you to enter. The building may have many doors, but usually just one is marked Entrance.

This is a simple concept that most men grasp easily. Every woman, except for your wife or future wife, is an exit sign. If you move toward another woman in a sexual manner, you are exiting God's best plan for your life. If you are married, you are for sure exiting God's one and only will for your life—your wife.

So when you're at the mall, department store, restaurant, or even church, and you find yourself looking at someone inappropriately, just imagine an exit sign over her head. If you're objectifying or lusting after a woman, imagine an exit sign at the top of her head so you know that you are exiting God's best and moving onto the ramp taking you to the road to trouble.

The entrance sign is just as important to understand as the exit sign. Your wife, and only your wife (or future wife), is the entrance sign to all God's blessings for you. Regardless of what mood she is currently in, she is the only entrance for your romantic and sexual expression. I know there are challenging days; remember I am not only a psychologist but I am also a husband and father of a daughter. People are not perfect, but you can be certain you are in God's will when being romantic and sexual toward your wife.

The next time you look at your wife, try imagining an entrance sign over her head. This can shift your mood, reminding you that she is a gift to you for now and the future. You deserve God's best, and his best is to stay on the road with your spouse or future spouse with as good an attitude as possible.

7. Praise and Touch

After professionally counseling many men, I can say without any reservations that the vast majority of men feel loved and appreciated by being praised and physically touched. If you are like most of us, this is an issue you will have to address, or it can leave you vulnerable as a single or married man.

If you're married, talk to your wife about your need to be touched. If you ask for sex every time she tries to be affectionate, you have to take responsibility for your wife not being that excited to touch you because she's thinking she doesn't always want to have sex. So separate the needs for touch and sex. Ask to be touched, but separate this so that touching you is safe for your wife.

There are women who find touch challenging. They may be abuse survivors, may have had unaffectionate parents, or might feel you're overly needy to desire so much touch. This kind of woman may also be an intimacy anorexic, which we will talk more about later. In that case, she is intentionally not touching you because she knows you like it and it would bring you closer to her. Intimacy anorexics desire a certain amount of distance in their marriages.

If you appeal to your wife and she refuses to meet your desire for touch, get help. Go together to a pastor, mentor couple, or counselor. If she is starving for intimacy because you don't pray or share your heart, give her a safe place to vent. If, however, it is her issue, offer her a place to grow.

If your wife totally rejects help, then find a safe, licensed, reputable, massage therapist of a gender you both agree on, whom your wife meets and feels comfortable with, and schedule regular sessions to meet this need. If your need is met in a healthy way, you are less vulnerable, if a woman touches or hugs you randomly, to interpret it in a sexual manner.

Praise is also important to men. Before you ask your wife for praise, first ask how often and what type of praise you are sowing into your wife's heart. Are you praising who she is, or just what she does? Are you giving praise with enthusiasm or in a monotone voice? From whom do you hear words like, *Great job; you're smart, kind, creative, hardworking*? If this is mostly outside of your marriage, talk to your wife. You might want to follow Lisa's and my example: I give her two praises a day and she gives me two praises a day. This keeps both of our needs for praise a priority.

Be wise about who you let praise or touch you on a regular basis. Women know that men like praise and touch, and some will use this knowledge to seduce you. If a woman praises me, I am cautious. If she continues, I am extremely cautious because deep down I know I'm not really that amazing. As a married man, if a woman touches me, especially if it's on a regular basis, I definitely set clear boundaries.

8. Respect

Respect is a core issue for men. Wives are told to respect their husbands, but honestly some men make that difficult. If you don't keep your word, provide financially, keep up with home projects, pray with her, help around the house, and try to love her the way she wants to be loved, then it will be hard for her to respect you. Ask yourself if your behavior around the house and toward your wife is truly respectable. If the answer is no, you are creating a very difficult environment in which your wife is to respect you. You need respect; but if you are not giving respect by serving well, you are creating a wife who nags and criticizes, and you will feel less respected.

First, work on the respect you're showing your wife and on your behavior around the house. Then define for yourself what respect looks like. If you think it is obedience, you are too immature to be respected. Try again, and think about what would make you feel respected. Then talk to your wife about it. If you get nowhere, talk to a mentor couple, pastor, or counselor to have this issue resolved, so that respect is a common commodity in your marriage.

If your respect needs are mostly getting met outside

your marriage, you are vulnerable to any female's respect. Please address this issue so you don't find yourself walking down the road to trouble.

9. Daily Declaration

I find it helpful to make a daily commitment to stay on the right road and avoid the road to trouble. I accept that I am at war, not just with the devil and this very sexual culture, but also with myself. James 1:14 says that we are drawn away by our own lust. That means that left to myself, I could lust, I could think higher of myself than I should, or feel entitled to a better wife, life, or something else. I am like you—in a battle of my own flesh.

Here is something I have learned to do to declare war on my flesh. As part of my prayer in the morning many times before my feet even hit the floor, I declare a few commitments to the Lord. I declare that I commit to love and protect all women today, that I hate all lust of all women in my heart or my mind, and that all women are made by God, for God, and going back to God.

This daily declaration has put a stake in the ground deep inside me—I can't explain it. It's as though I've told myself how the day is going to be. If I am tempted to look twice at a woman, a voice inside asks, "Are you protecting her?" This daily declaration tells my flesh that today I am focused on winning any battle that comes up in this area. I make this declaration even if I am going to be hanging out at home with Lisa all day.

10. Prayer: The Word and the War

Prayer is a critical part of staying off the road to trouble. Praying daily is essential for a Christian man, whether on your knees, in your truck, with hands up or down. Connecting to God, praising him, and listening to him are critical to walking in any spiritual strength.

Reading, memorizing, listening to, and meditating on the Bible is important to staying strong. I not only read the Bible but I also like to listen to it on CD on my drive to work. Revelation from the Word is sweet and strengthening. When we fear God in a respectful manner, we want to pray and read his Word.

I am so saddened by men who only hear, "You have to pray and read your Bible," when I talk to them. These men have no clue that we *get* to pray and glean wisdom from the Bible. As a lost person, I had no desire for these behaviors. As a believer, I know that it's a privilege to pray and read the Word.

11. Hero in One Story

Men love a good epic hero story. You know, the classic theme of a good guy getting into some conflict or trouble. He then meets Merlin or Mickey Mouse or gets the magic power, gem, or formula, and fights the good fight, defeats the foe, gets the beautiful woman, and obtains the kingdom.

These are heroic, epic literature themes. In the real world, heroes are limited to one story each. There are millions of maidens in distress (note to single guys—they are in distress for a reason). You and I can only be a hero in one woman's story. You guessed it: the story of your wife or future wife is the only place you can be a hero. I can't be a hero to the single mom, single woman, woman in a bad marriage, or divorced woman, rich or poor. No matter what situation a woman may be in, I am not able to be her hero. That job belongs to God and a man who can commit his whole life to that role. An exception to this might be if your wife dies, you could then be a hero to another woman you would commit your life to.

I can only be a hero to Lisa and my children, and you can only be a hero to your wife and family. If I want to be a hero, I will work through my marriage and family issues. I die to myself, serve well, get scars, and stay off the road to trouble and on the clean road God has marked out for me to travel.

As we travel this road alongside our wives and God, we can experience an incredible journey together. For those who have failed along the way and have experienced the consequences for that failure, it's not too late to become the hero in your story. Our church and culture are depending on you and me to be heroes to those we love in the name of Christ so that our sons and daughters can see and believe that they too can be future heroes.

The Two-Sided Problem

There are two sides to a big problem that exists in the church today. The first side we have talked about is the issue of lust and inappropriate sexual behavior. The second is more insidious and is silently killing our marriages. I call this intimacy anorexia and in this chapter hope to shed light on this issue, which is impacting many Christian marriages. I have spent many years traveling and speaking at men's and marriage conferences. I have spoken in most denominations, to Catholics and Protestants, and to hundreds and thousands of men at a time in almost every state in the union and in other nations as well. I have asked a particular question to the men in these various settings and received the same response universally.

While I am closing a session, I'll say something like, "Many of you have been listening to all this talk about sex, pornography, and the issues most of us face. Now, I want to ask you a question tonight. How many of you are not struggling? Maybe you're way past struggling. You've tried, cried, and prayed to get free for years or decades, and you're addicted? I want you to raise your hand tonight."

Half or more of the men's hands will go up every time. I'm certain that some men can't raise their hands because of the guilt or shame they are feeling. If 50 percent of the brothers in the body of Christ have sexual addictions, we will do well to understand how to identify an addiction and what to do about it if it is. Even if you've not looked at one image of pornography, you need to read this chapter. Every man needs this information if we are going to have the men in the church get and stay clean for their entire lives.

How can you know if something, anything, is an addiction, whether it's alcohol, drugs, work, porn, or sex? Here are several characteristics of an addiction, and you can apply each to sexual addiction. Some of these ideas I'm sharing are from my books *The Final Freedom: Pioneering Sexual Addiction Recovery* and *Intimacy Anorexia: Healing the Hidden Addiction in Your Marriage.*[1]

Characteristics of Addiction

1. **Effort.** This man has made attempts to stop his fantasy, pornography, masturbation, or acting out

with others. He may have been motivated inter-
nally to stop, or externally by being caught. Regardless, these efforts repeatedly end up in failure.

2. **Read My Lips.** Remember when President George
H. W. Bush made that promise to not raise taxes and
then later he did exactly what he said he wouldn't
do? The addict has made promises to himself, his
wife, girlfriend, pastor, friend, or accountability
partner to stop. He, however, keeps breaking this
promise to himself or others.

3. **Consequences.** As the addiction grows, consequences occur. These consequences may be a bad
marriage, getting caught, getting arrested, being
separated, divorce, losing a job, having a ruined
reputation, getting STDs, being blackmailed, or
it could be as simple as the constant guilt, shame,
anxiety, or depression a man experiences when living a double life.

4. **Keeping It Going.** Even after consequences that are
sometimes severe, this man goes back to his sexually inappropriate behavior. It seems insane to go
back after such consequences, but the addicted
man does exactly that.

5. **Do More.** Doing more is simply increasing the
frequency or intensity of the addictive behavior.
For the man who uses pornography, this means

he might increase his hours of use. He might go from occasional to daily to hours a day over the course of time.

6. **Takes More.** For the addicted man, it begins to take more and more to get the same effect. What once was an occasional flirt with pornography can grow into more perverse forms of pornography or acting out behaviors. It can also go from using porn to using people and then to all types of attempts to do more risky or perverted sex acts to get the same buzz he used to get from just a little pornography.

7. **More Preoccupation.** All addictions are behaviors that take time to perform. As the addiction grows in a man's life, it takes more time for him on a daily, weekly, or monthly basis. It becomes your preoccupation, your hobby. As an addict you preoccupy yourself by spending more time to pursue a behavior or person, then more time with that behavior or person, and maybe even more time recovering from the behaviors or events with these people.

8. **The Blues.** As a man increases his dependence on his addiction to deal with his current or past issues, it is very common for him to feel withdrawals when the drug isn't present or available. These cycles may include guilt or shame, or they may feel like a very strong hunger to act out. Withdrawals for the

sex addict are real and tend to go into remission in increments of thirty days after the last acting out has occurred.

9. **Decreasing Other Activities.** As the addict grows in his addiction, other things in his life must get smaller. The addict will have less time for his wife, family, recreation, social or vocational activities. His interest in real life diminishes as the desires for more of the addictive behavior increases.

Review these characteristics for a moment. On a separate sheet of paper, mark down any of the categories that you may be currently experiencing. For those of you who don't struggle, you might want to put these characteristics in your phone so you can help other guys figure out if they are addicted or not.

1. Effort
2. Read My Lips
3. Consequences
4. Keeping It Going
5. Do More
6. Takes More (of the behavior)
7. More Preoccupation
8. The Blues / Withdrawal
9. Decreasing Other Activities

If you said yes to three or more of these characteristics to any behavior in your life, you are probably addicted. If you said yes to three or more of these characteristics about a specific sexual behavior, then you could easily make this statement, "My name is _____, and I am a sex addict."

You can theologize, philosophize, whine, or complain, but you will still have a sexual addiction. Just be honest and look at the track record you have on being successful at getting and staying clean. There is no shame in admitting the truth. If you are a recovering sex addict, it doesn't make God become any less God; it makes him more as you walk the road to recovery together.

For men who have never struggled in this area, thank you for taking the time to read through this. Many of your Christian brothers are struggling and about half are addicted.

If you are addicted, I encourage you to take this seriously for you and your family's sake. The principles in this book can help you in general but you will need a regimen to walk out of this addiction. You will have to be more militant against the addiction than the man who just occasionally struggles. Because of this I am adding ideas here that are more specifically geared toward addiction recovery. Every man should read through here so you can help someone else who is a sexual addict even if you aren't.

Another recovery step you can utilize is known in our Christian recovery circle as the 5 Cs. The 5 Cs, or the Five Commandments, are a set of five daily recovery behaviors that you or someone you may be helping can apply. These five basic behaviors, if done for the first ninety days of getting and staying clean, can be extremely effective. Let me list and briefly explain each one.

5 Commandments (5 Cs)

1. **Pray.** Each day, start with prayer. Specifically ask God to help you stay clean today. This sets your day ready to connect to God and also helps you accept your reliance on God to get and stay clean today.

2. **Read.** I am all for reading the Bible, and every Christian man does well to read the Bible daily to grow spiritually. In this context, *read* means to read literature or books on sexual addiction recovery. These books can encourage you and keep you focused on getting clean during the first few important months of the journey.

3. **Meetings.** Get into a group with men who are specifically addressing the issue of sex addiction. I recommend Freedom groups because they are work groups, not just support groups. In a Freedom

group, unlike a support group, you can be given direct feedback. You will also check in on the recovery work accomplished and your level of freedom every week. In traditional support groups, you don't have to do any work and nobody really knows if you are sober or not. Because Freedom groups are work groups, they have been found to be significantly more effective in helping men get and stay clean.

4. **Calls.** In Freedom groups, daily phone calls are expected to be made to other group members for the first ninety days. You check in every day to build your team up, and if you are struggling that day, you call other guys first before you act out. It's also a time to process what you are doing in your 101 Freedom workbook or Steps to Freedom workbook for your recovery. The whole team is calling each other, so winning is much easier for each member.

5. **Pray Again.** In the evening you also pray, thanking God for a day of being clean. You thank him because he not only has given you the grace and strength to be clean, he also has given you a team and real tools to stay clean, and that is something to be totally grateful for on a daily basis.

For any man who realizes he's addicted, please set a goal to be clean. It really can happen if you take the time to work these principles. Many fail because they never tell anyone about their struggle or never attend a group. If your church doesn't have a group, even if you never struggled, start a group. Men will come, and many who come to these groups will be born leaders, so leadership will not be difficult to turn over to one of them once they start getting clean.

Every church can be a hospital station for the sexually addicted men in the body of Christ. A man with the freedom tools can lead a group anywhere. Please, seriously pray about being that man and being a solution where you are.

The Other Side of the Coin

Now let's discuss another side of the problem. This part of the problem will show up in marriages. I would encourage singles to read this section just to be informed about this side of the coin. In our research on sexual addiction, we have found that approximately one-third of the men who are sexual addicts who are married have a second major issue. We have also found out that about 40 percent of the wives of sexual addicts have this same problem. The real difficulty is that neither of them knows they have the problem, and it can make getting and staying free a lot more difficult. Here are a few example of how it works.

Jake is a really nice guy at church. His neighbors love

him, and so do the people in the political party where he volunteers. Jake is dependable for everyone—everyone but his wife, Emily. Jake publicly praises Emily and puts his arm around her in public, but at home he rarely touches her or praises her.

Jake is too busy to date his wife, and he does not have time for deep conversations. Even sex has taken a backseat and occurs less and less frequently. At home, Jake is critical toward Emily and often blames her for any problem that comes up in their marriage. He rarely shares feelings other than anger and doesn't initiate prayer with her at home, but he does participate in altar-call duty every Sunday.

Jossie and Roger have been married twenty-seven years. Jossie has always struggled with giving Roger physical attention or praise. He says he can't do anything right or good enough for her. Roger wants to take Jossie out for a date, but she's tired or busy with her multilevel business. Jossie won't pray with Roger because "she's a private person." In twenty-seven years, Jossie has only initiated sex once after having some wine at a wedding, and she hasn't had wine since.

She complains about Roger's job and his weight, and she stays angry with Roger in such a way that she controls him by her moods. Jossie also makes twice as much money as Roger, and she shames him if he buys anything for himself, while there are no restraints to her spending. Publicly Jossie is affectionate, but at home Roger can't remember the last time she gave him a kiss or said "I love you" without being asked, or not in return after he says it.

What's wrong in these marriages? They all love Jesus and go to church. One huge issue is that up until now, they didn't have a name for their problem. Both of these couples struggle with what we call *intimacy anorexia*.

Again, some of you will never have had a day of struggling with this issue. However, if a man or couple you know is struggling with this and you give them a language or paradigm to understand what they are experiencing, they can start to address and solve it.

Intimacy anorexia is the active withholding of emotional, spiritual, and sexual intimacy from the spouse. That means, and this is challenging to accept, that one spouse is intentionally withholding various aspects of him- or herself from the other spouse. It's as if the intimacy anorexic is married to themselves and creates ongoing distance from their husband or wife.

If a man is struggling with sexual addiction and intimacy anorexia, it is very important he works on both issues at the same time; otherwise he may be vulnerable to relapse and not totally understand why he is relapsing.

Let me give you a brief summary of the characteristics of intimacy anorexia. These characteristics can help you identify this issue in yourself or in the lives of others you may know.

Characteristics of Intimacy Anorexia

1. **Busy.** Intimacy anorexics stay so busy that they have little time for their spouses. They can be busy with house projects, volunteering, the computer, television, video games, or reading the paper. Their spouse feels very alone in the marriage and often even their pets get more attention than the spouse does.

2. **Blame.** Intimacy anorexics will blame their spouses for the problems in the marriage. They want to be seen as all good, all the time; and therefore if it's not good, it's the spouse's fault.

3. **Withholding Love.** The intimacy anorexic actively withholds love in the way the spouse likes to be loved. If it's touch, the spouse won't give it. If it's gifts that make the spouse feel special, that person won't buy them gifts. When an intimacy anorexic realizes that the relationship is in serious trouble, however, he or she knows exactly what to do to show love and get back into good graces. Intimacy anorexics know what to do; they just intentionally and routinely don't do it for their spouses.

4. **Withholding Praise.** Intimacy anorexics do not regularly praise their spouses privately. In public, the spouses might get praise, but at home, day in and

day out, there is an intentional lack of praise. It's not that the anorexics do not know the great qualities of their spouses; it's that they won't speak these positive thoughts to them.

5. **Withholding Sex.** Not all intimacy anorexics withhold sex from their spouses. Most intimacy anorexics do, though, withhold intimacy during sex. He or she might be fantasizing about something or just be disconnected. Some anorexics withhold sex by not initiating it, not talking about sex, or having no creativity about sex, although some actually withhold sex.

6. **Withholding Spiritually.** Intimacy anorexics can be very religious by attending church and sometimes even being the pastor or spiritual leader at the church. At home they rarely pray with their spouses, or worship, or read the Bible together. Individually they do their spiritual thing, but they withhold their spirituality from their husband or wife.

7. **Feelings.** Intimacy anorexics are unwilling or unable to share their feelings with their spouses. When it comes to feelings, they will avoid these conversations or go blank or silent when feelings come up.

8. **Criticism.** Ongoing or ungrounded criticism is another characteristic of intimacy anorexia. This

characteristic can flare up if the couple is getting close, or when closeness would be expected, like on vacation.

9. **Anger or Silence.** An intimacy anorexic can use anger or silence to control the other spouse. I know couples who literally didn't speak to each other for weeks. I also know other anorexics who use anger to keep the other spouse at a certain distance.

10. **Money.** This is the least common feature of intimacy anorexia, but when it's present, it is strong. The intimacy anorexic will use money to control the spouse. This can happen in several ways, including giving the spouse an allowance, making the spouse have to ask for money, intentionally keeping the spouse ignorant of money issues, or letting him or her buy anything as long as they don't ask for intimacy.

Take the Test

Often intimacy anorexics are in denial about these behaviors, so I have a unique way in which I want you to answer these questions. The first set asks how your spouse would rate you on the following characteristics. Would your spouse say yes or no if they were asked these questions about how they believe you relate to them? On a separate sheet of paper, write out what their responses would be.

My wife would say:

1. I stay so busy that I have little time for her.
2. When issues come up, my first reflex or response is to blame her.
3. I withhold love from her when issues come up.
4. I withhold praise from her.
5. I withhold sex from her or am not present during sex.
6. I withhold spiritual connection from her.
7. I am unwilling or unable to share my authentic feelings with her.
8. I use anger or silence to control her.
9. I have ongoing or ungrounded criticism (spoken or unspoken) toward her.
10. I control or shame her regarding money or spending.

Second, I want you to answer these questions about your spouse. Use a separate piece of paper and just put yes or no on it.

I would say my wife:

1. Stays so busy that she has little time for me.
2. Blames me as her first reflex when issues come up.

3. Withholds love from me.

4. Withholds praise from me.

5. Withholds sex from me or is not present during sex.

6. Withholds spiritual connection from me.

7. Is unwilling or unable to share her authentic feelings with me.

8. Uses anger or silence to control me.

9. Has ongoing or ungrounded criticism (spoken or unspoken) toward me.

10. Controls or shames me regarding money or spending

Count the number of yes answers that you put down on your score for her, and also her score for you. If one or both of you have five or more yes answers, you have probably been dealing with intimacy anorexia without knowing it.

If you and your spouse scored low, great! Just being aware of this information can make you more helpful to other couples from here on. If, however, this does apply to you, please get informed by reading helpful materials or getting professional counseling.

I love seeing men get clean. Some need to put the brakes on the sexual acting out, but also put their feet on the accelerator to reconnect and stay connected to their wives. Many

Christian men's books on this topic seem to want to minimize sexual addiction rather than eradicating it. But once you know what sexual addiction is, you can get and stay clean. My prayer is that you would find solutions if either of these two-sided issues fit for you. Regardless, I hope I can in some way encourage you to be part of the solution for your local church.

13

Staying on Offense

It's 6:00 a.m. as I pen this final chapter. Today is not a normal day. Later today, many millions of people will be watching two football teams play their division championship game, just one step from the Super Bowl.

Sports are great for us men. Playing them offers many character-building qualities. You learn discipline, thinking bigger than yourself, sacrifice, commitment, and so much more. As the game plays today, we all know exactly what the commentators are going to be talking about more often than each player's performance and statistics. They are going to be talking about the teams' offense and defense.

Most sports, not just football, have defensive and offensive strategies. When you have the ball, puck, or whatever it is, you're on offense. When on offense, you are penetrating the enemy's territory trying to score a point of some type.

When you are on defense, the other team has the ball or puck, and you are doing everything you possibly can to prevent them from scoring. That's the way it works in sports and in life: back and forth.

In the first chapter, we looked at how our enemy has declared war. We also looked at several statistics regarding how pornography and other sexually inappropriate behaviors are growing in the church of Jesus Christ, affecting every church, in every denomination, in every city and town in our country.

We saw how the actions of men who participate in an unclean life hurt their wives and children. This impact on others increases the score, so to speak, of the enemy against our church and our culture.

Jesus warned us about losing our "saltiness" in Matthew 5:13, because if we lose our power as salt and light at this time in world history, it could be a big score for the enemy. Think of it this way: if the church gets more trapped by pornography and immorality, both before and after marriage, our culture doesn't stand a chance.

The enemy is after the prize, and our collective spiritual authority is the prize in this game. If he can continue to seduce the church worldwide, he will temporarily reduce our impact on the world. Our impact is the single reason the world is as good as it is today. Men, we are players on the other team. We can't play as if there is another game.

We can't afford to put anything less than 100 percent into the game we are in right now.

I have a passion for taking this land for Jesus, with sexually clean men in every church, from every denomination, in every town and city in our nation and beyond our borders. We can change the scoreboard in two major ways: by leading others to Christ and with our personal and church-wide offensive tactics.

Leading Others to Christ

Every time someone comes to Christ, that's the ultimate point. If you are living an unclean life, your passion for the lost becomes smaller as you have to focus on yourself. As you live a clean life, you become more aware of the blood and grace of Jesus Christ who saved you, and you want to lead others to Christ. Leading people to Christ is the ultimate offensive weapon.

Leading someone to Christ is easy. Just ask them, "If you died tonight, would you go to heaven?" If they're not sure, ask if they would like to be sure, and then ask them to pray with you, "Jesus, I ask you to forgive me of my sins. I accept your death, your blood as full payment for me, and receive your salvation. Come into my heart and lead me."

If you are reading this book and you have never accepted Jesus Christ as your personal Lord and Savior, stop reading and pray that prayer right now. If you start reading the Bible, start in the book of John, and find a local church to grow in.

Personal Tactics

The other way we stay on offense is personally and as a church. Personally, if you have sons, you stay on offense by talking to your sons preventatively and regularly. I don't use the excuse that because my dad didn't know what to do or say to me, I'm going to curse my son with the same experience. Talking to my son is my job, period. There are materials to help,[1] but in this battle we can't afford to lose our sons. We must be that generation of men who talk to our sons at least monthly about sexual issues to protect them from guilt, secrets, or shame. These young men are not only the hope for our families; they are also the hope of the church for generations to come.

Ask yourself, *If my son duplicates how I raised him regarding sexual purity, would I have strong or weak men down my sexual family tree?* I realize some of you are grandfathers and you didn't have information on how to do this. You can talk to your sons, daughters, sons-in-law, and daughters-in-law and ask them what they are doing. Or, if you do not have children, you can focus on someone you're in a position to mentor—ask your pastor, he most likely could use help mentoring men in this area. If they don't have a plan, offer to help. It's never too late to go on offense for our families and loved ones.

Staying on offense is asking your brother the tough questions. Remember the questions? "When was the last time you masturbated?" "When was the last time you looked at porn?" These questions need to become part of our Christian male culture. I believe men want to be asked, and men want to be clean. However, we lack men bold enough to inquire consistently and keep us accountable.

When you pull a man out of sexual secrecy into the light, you score a point against our enemy. I love seeing this happen because many of these men are already saved, but now they can be effective. I've had many conversations with men who have become better dads, husbands, and church members, and many have grown exponentially financially and in their field of influence.

Churchwide Tactics

When you score these kinds of points over years in your local church, it's the gift that keeps on giving. These men have multiple ministries, and their churches have become real hospital stations for the wounded and make winning players for our team. There are several issues to discuss while moving into corporate offense as a local church.

Teens

As teenagers, our children need really consistent, informative, frank discussions about sexual purity, STDs, and pregnancy. Our public schools not only inform our children about immorality of every kind and call it education, they almost promote it. You need to counter this aggressively.

You can also invite men and women speakers on a regular basis to speak to the youth about purity. I have done many of these talks, and the response is universal. The teens are grateful. They want to be told the truth and honestly want to live clean lives. In our youth groups, it's okay for the youth pastor or safe adults, both men and women, to have accountability time or groups with the teens. It's good for an approved person of the same gender to ask straight questions to our teens. As a precaution, churches should do screening checks on those in youth programs to prevent known pedophiles from access to youth groups. The safety and security of our children is paramount, and it is our responsibility to guard it in every situation—even on our home turf.

Singles

Many singles feel disconnected from the rest of the church. I am in favor of singles serving in every area of church. If you are single, you are an awesome blessing; your gifts and talents and time can be used in so many positive ways to advance God's kingdom. Singles also need sexual purity talks on a regular basis. They need regular accountability. I think accountability should be standard church culture, and each church should decide how they want this to look.

I strongly recommend that each church create a dating policy to outline what it expects from singles who want to date each other. Church leadership should create this policy and review it regularly. If you need an outline, check out our DVD *Successfully Single*.[2] You'll find an individual dating policy that outlines the process of dating and accountability. This is something a single person should look at to make decisions to avoid sexual immorality in the church. There is also a physical-affection-boundaries sheet singles can walk through to determine length of time in a relationship before certain affection acts occur.

Singles can break up into same-gender groups and review their boundaries. It's important to do this on a regular basis, inoculating them and cleaning up small issues before they become large issues. A fun thing to do with singles is to ask everyone to get their cell phones out and lift them up. Then ask them to keep them up if they have access to the Internet on their phones. To those who don't put their hands down, I ask how many have accountability software like Covenant Eyes that offers Internet activity reports to an accountability partner. Now all the phones left are "dumb phones," not smartphones. It isn't smart at all to have an open porn store 24–7 in your pocket or purse.

As a point of technological accountability, are the singles' pastors or mature friends on their social network sites? What are the boundaries for accepting new friends on their social sites? Predators love naïve young Christian people. Both heterosexual and homosexual predators look for the lonely and naïve, and we should look at singles as a group the whole church needs to protect.

A church can consider mentor couples to walk with singles. Adopting singles is helpful, especially for the empty nesters. These mentor relationships can be life changing for our single people.

Engaged Couples

Engaged couples profit immensely from having a mentor couple holding them accountable for physical boundaries in a caring way. It gets tough physically as you move toward marriage. In premarital counseling, couples should discuss their sexual pasts and address sexual abuse, pornography, or sexual addiction issues.

Set these couples up for real success by having them practice the sharing of feelings, praying together, and serving together in a local church. I recommend the church have some structured reading in preparation for marriage.

Married Couples

Married couples also need the sexual purity message. This is best done by others of the same gender. Women need to be talked to about the danger of online relationships, boundaries with other men, how to spot a man who wants to hurt their marriages, inappropriate books, television shows, and movies, and pornography. We live in a day in which the enemy is trying to take down our wives.

Married men need the same accountability as singles, by having accountability partners as standard experience in our churches, as we've spoken about throughout this book. Everyone feels safer in a church where men are accountable. Men need regular sexual purity and boundaries conversations as well. A church that doesn't talk about this is scoring points for the enemy as its men quietly suffer.

A church on offense is one that communicates to its men regularly. This kind of church has an "ask and tell policy," not a "don't ask, don't tell policy." This is a different day, and we as a church must adapt to the battle. Married men need the accountability software that gives reports to their wives as well. Lisa, my wife, has Covenant Eyes on our home computer; nobody gets in trouble on our computer. Married men need this type of protection on their cell phones as well. As silly as it sounds, I like Covenant Eyes' little eye icon that pops up on my computer and phone. I haven't looked at porn for more than twenty-five years, but that icon reminds me that God is watching, and so are the cloud of witnesses mentioned in Hebrews 12:1.

Church Leadership

The church leadership can also decide if "don't ask, don't tell" is acceptable for hiring new church pastoral and leadership staff. I support asking potential candidates about pornography, masturbation, and infidelity up front. I am even agreeable to pastors in key positions taking a polygraph to verify their sexual purity for the last couple of years, making sure pornography, masturbation, and infidelity are not part of their lives.

A church on the offense protects its congregation from sexually impure leadership. These proactive steps can keep the enemy from scoring points. Leaders can shut down a church or severely damage it for years or decades if they go through a scandal of this type. Your church doesn't have to suffer through this, and it's good prevention to trust but verify candidates for leadership.

Groups

Let's go another step further in staying on the offense. Every church has what it takes to start being a solution for our culture and the body of Christ in their city.

In every local church, I have found the antibodies for this cancer—men and women who are willing to lead structured support groups. We call these groups Freedom groups for the men. Local churches have renamed them Purity groups, Clean groups, and Valor groups. We are not concerned about what it's called, we simply want men having weekly accountability, working through the Freedom group material, calling each other, and getting and staying clean for a lifetime.

The other antibodies are these men's wives. The residual damage of living with a man who has lived an unclean sexual life can be significant. We call groups for these women Partners groups, but again, different churches have called them many creative names. Our group works through the *Partners* book and other recovery material, including the *Partners Recovery Guide* and *Beyond Love*.[3] The women in these groups call each other throughout the week and experience amazing healing.

Every church has rooms it is not using during the week. The church could open its building up on an evening or Saturday morning. My experience is that when a church starts a group, they expect their church members to make up most of the participants. That rarely happens. Instead, church people from all over town will come to these groups. The church can be a citywide ministry to those the enemy has damaged.

When a lost person needs help with a sexual addiction or a wife needs support, and you are there surrounding them with Christians, guess what? They get saved and then start attending the church that was there for them in their hour of need.

Counselors

If your church has the luxury of having an onsite counselor, please encourage him or her to become a certified sexual recovery therapist (SRT) through the American Association for Sex Addiction Therapy.[4] They are required to view forty-five hours of DVDs that include more than two hundred academic references. This training has been used in a major university in Colorado as a master's level online counseling course. Then they have six months of supervision with an AASAT supervisor. And then they are certified. Many of the counselors, during their six-month supervision, doubled their practice or needed to add more counselors to their team. Once people find out there is real help, they show up.

If you have someone who has a heart for this type of ministry but isn't a licensed counselor, they can become a sexual recovery coach (SRC). A sexual recovery coach goes through two processes. He or she does life coach training through an approved, designated organization, and then takes the AASAT course of forty-five hours with six months of supervision. This can be helpful for someone who has the heart and gifting to help others, but not the time available that it would take to get a degree.

Staying on the offense, individually and corporately, is what it is going to take to win this game. Our opponent may seem to be ahead, but I know God is raising a standard above what we currently see.

During the last twenty-five years, I have seen the church at large move from a place of total denial that there even was a problem to looking for solutions. Some of the denominations have created their own materials, and that's great. Local churches, independent of each other, all across the country have started support groups of all types. A national organization called Celebrate Recovery embraced sexual addiction recovery and provided a great model of organization, which is a huge plus for the body of Christ.

Within the last fifteen years, more and more pastors started including this area of struggle in their sermons and altar calls. Counselors like me are being called upon to speak at conferences and professional training sessions all over the world. Large television ministries are embracing this need.

I am encouraged so much by the growth I have seen in churches, and how they help men get and stay clean. I am excited that many of you men feel that call to arms, and in your own way, lay down your lives for your brothers and their families. I can smell freedom coming into our church in a new way, all across the country and world. It's a freedom that is clean from sexual impurity, a reinvigoration of sexual purity and authority for all age groups in the church.

I know Jesus is coming back for his church. I, like you, want to be part of his team to clean up the church so she is ready for his return.

You are the solution for yourself, your family, your church, and our culture. I have seen God rescue men from some pretty horrible pits, and I have seen these men become truly godly men and leaders. In my office, I have a group of men who volunteer to lead our Freedom groups who were each trapped in sexual addiction years ago. In our leaders meeting recently, I highlighted to them that not only did we have close to seventy years of freedom jointly, that they have now become men who care that their brothers get and stay clean their entire lives. It's remarkable, and encouraging.

Healing the Lepers

My wish for you, whether you struggle with these issues or not, is that you would get in the battle. Many of you are familiar with the story of Jesus healing the ten lepers:

> As he was going into a village, ten men who had leprosy met him. They stood at a distance and called out in a loud voice, "Jesus, Master, have pity on us!" When he saw them, he said, "Go, show yourselves to the priests." And as they went, they were cleansed. (Luke 17:12–14)

There are principles to healing the lepers that are appropriate for men who want to get and stay clean. The first principle is *desperation*. These lepers were not in denial about being lepers. This is important because if a man stays in denial, he cannot move to become clean, and his uncleanness grows and grows. If you have a sexual issue that is beating you up, please, please don't stay in denial. That is not an offense move in your life, and many are depending on you.

Second, these men *went to Jesus*. Remember our conversation about James and John? I strongly encourage each man to have a relationship with Jesus and the Jesus who lives in his brothers.

Third, Jesus declared they were healed when he told them to go *show themselves* to the priest, so the men had to do two things. They had to hear, even in their leper state, the word of Jesus that they were healed of this dreadful disease. These men not only had to hear the word; they had to obey the word. If any of them did not obey, they risked quite a bit. Then they had to submit to authority. The priest was the only one who could legally determine if they were truly clean. These men had to be inspected, and after they heard the word *clean* from the priest, they could return to their communities.

We can read deeper into this story to discover a tale about a man we will call Levi, which will demonstrate these principles in a more vivid way. Levi was a young man who worked in the fields for his family's food. He was strong, handsome, and loved his Jewish wife. Levi was a faithful man in his local synagogue. Levi's rabbi was named Eli. Eli had known Levi since he was born; he had circumcised him as the law required. Levi lived close by the synagogue while growing up, so he often helped with small things around the synagogue.

Eli was like an uncle to Levi. When it was time for Levi to marry, he could think of no one better to marry him than his betrothed, Leah. Eli married Levi and Leah, and within a few years their two sons were born. Life was good for years for Levi, working hard and watching his boys grow.

Then something began to happen to Levi. He began to act peculiar. He stopped playing with the boys, he was tired more often than usual, and he began to sit in the back of the synagogue and come late and leave early. He would not sleep with Leah and also wouldn't take off his outer garment, not even at home.

Leah told her concerns to Eli, and he promised to talk to the young man. It took a few weeks for Eli to catch him before leaving and ask to talk to him. Levi agreed. At their scheduled time to meet, however, Levi didn't show. Eli knew this wasn't like Levi; he had always been like a faithful son he could depend on.

Eli knew he was going to have to visit Levi. He set it up with Leah for her to be out of the house, and Eli would wait for him there. When Levi walked through the door, he was not only startled but looked deeply afraid when he saw Eli waiting for him.

Eli said to Levi, "Something's wrong, Levi, tell me what it is."

Levi said, "Nothing, just tired, getting older."

Eli said, "Levi, take off your garment."

Levi said, "No. Please, no."

Eli insisted, "Son, take off your garment. I command you."

Levi started to cry and asked him to please not ask him to do this, but Eli insisted. Levi's body had sores, as Eli expected. Eli's job was to inspect, and Levi knew this. Eli said the word that changed Levi's life: *"Unclean."*

Levi had leprosy. The word *unclean* sent Levi running from his house, knowing he could never come back, never go to work, never be with his wife. Every time Levi came within a certain distance of a person, he was required to shout the very word Eli spoke over his life: *unclean.*

As time went on, Levi began to hate Eli for pronouncing him unclean. He became not only sick in body but also bitter in spirit. A rumor reached the group of lepers that Levi had become a part of—there was a man who could heal lepers. His name was Jesus, and he was coming to their town.

Ten of them, including Levi, went to seek out this Jesus. They found him and he told them to go show themselves to the priest. As they walked, they became healthier, stronger, and their skin was healing faster than they could believe.

Levi was running to his village, but then stopped. He realized the priest he had to see was Eli, the same man who had spoken the word *unclean*. He knew only Eli could examine him, so he could go back to work and see his sons and family again.

Other healed lepers were ahead of Levi and they were leaving the priest shouting and screaming, "Clean! I'm clean!" Then Levi arrived. Eli, with tears in his eyes said, "Son, take off your garment," the very words he had used before. Levi, feeling bitterness and hope at the same time, took off his shirt. Eli inspected him as he did the others. Eli took Levi's face in his hands. This was the boy he had circumcised, given in marriage, and loved like a son. Eli looked right into Levi's eyes and said the words that would change both their lives: *"Clean, clean, clean; you are clean!"*

The men wept deeply, embracing and crying. Levi asked Eli to forgive him for blaming him. Eli forgave him, saying again, "You are clean, my son! You are clean!"

That's what I want every man reading this book to hear and say: "Clean! I am clean!"

Notes

Introduction

1. Tom Landry, *Tom Landry: An Autobiography* (Grand Rapids: Zondervan, 1990), 269.

Chapter 1: A Dirty War Declared

1. Jerry Ropelato, "Internet Pornography Statistics," Top Ten Reviews, accessed July 20, 2012, http://internet-filter-review.toptenreviews .com/internet-pornography-statistics.html.
2. P. J. Wright, "U.S. Males and Pornography, 1873–2010: Consumption, Predictors, Correlates," *Journal of Sex Research* (2011), doi: 10, 1–12.
3. K. Luck, "Living with Sexual Integrity," seminar presented at the Christian Camping International Conference, Vancouver, BC, December 1, 2009.
4. C. J. Gardner, "Tangled in the Worst of the Web," *Christianity Today*, 45, no. 4 (2001): 42–49; E. Reed, "Hooked: first he turned on the computer, then the computer turned on him," *Leadership* 22, no. 1 (2001); 86–94, as quoted in LynnAnne M. Joiner, "Congregants' Responses to Clergy Pornography Addiction," (PhD diss., Texas Tech University, 2008), 6.

5. Douglas Weiss, informal survey of 58 pastors at the National Coalition for the Protection of Children and Families, Cincinnati, Ohio, 2000.
6. "The Leadership Survey: Pastors Viewing Internet Pornography," *Leadership Journal*, 22, no. 1 (2001): 87–89.
7. J. Peter and P. M. Valkenburg, "Adolescents' Exposure to Sexually Explicit Online Material and Recreational Attitudes Toward Sex," *Journal of Communication*, 56, no. 4 (2006): 639–60, as cited in Deborah Braun-Courville and Mary Rojas, "Exposure to Sexually Explicit Web Sites and Adolescent Sexual Attitudes and Behaviors" *Journal of Adolescent Health*, 45 (2009): 156–62; see also E. Seidman, "The Pretreat: Contemporary Patterns of Pornography Use and the Psychodynamic Meaning of Frequent Pornography Use for Heterosexual Men," *Dissertation Abstract International: Section B: The Sciences and Engineering*, 64, no. 8-B (2004): 4063.
8. *Pornography's Impact on Marriage and the Family: Hearing before the Subcommittee on the Constitution, Civil Rights and Property, Committee on Judiciary, United States Senate*, 105th Cong. (2005) (Testimony of Jill C. Manning for the Heritage Foundation), accessed July 26, 2012, http://www.heritage.org/Research /Testimony/Pornographys-Impact-on-Marriage-amp-The-Family.
9. We gathered the information from a survey by the National Campaign to Prevent Teen and Unplanned Pregnancy and CosmoGirl.com. You can see the information at http://www.thenationalcampaign .org/sextech/pdf/sextech_summary.pdf.

Chapter 5: U + P = D

1. Douglas Weiss, *Partners: Healing from His Addiction* (Colorado Springs: Discovery Press, 1998).
2. Douglas Weiss, excerpts from *Beyond the Bedroom: Healing for Adult Children of Sex Addicts* (Colorado Springs: Discovery Press, 2005).
3. From Weiss, *Partners: Healing from His Addiction* (Discovery Press, 2011).
4. Ibid.
5. Ibid.
6. Ibid.

Chapter 6: Clean Brain

1. *Session 5: Biological Sex Addict,* American Association for Sex Addiction Therapy, DVD. Available at www.aasat.org.
2. Ibid.
3. Douglas Weiss, *The Final Freedom: Pioneering Sexual Addiction Recovery* (Colorado Springs: Discovery Press, 1998).

Chapter 12: The Two-Sided Problem

1. Douglas Weiss, *The Final Freedom: Pioneering Sexual Addiction Recovery* (Colorado Springs: Discovery Press, 2008). Douglas Weiss, *Intimacy Anorexia: Healing the Hidden Addiction in Your Marriage* (Colorado Springs, Discovery Press, 2010).

Chapter 13: Staying on Offense

1. Born for War: Porn Free Teens and Abstinence Clearing House
2. *Successfully Single* (2011; Colorado Springs, CO: Discovery Press), DVD.
3. Douglas Weiss, *Partners: Healing from His Addiction;* Weiss, *Partners Recovery Guide* (Colorado Springs: Discovery Press, 2011); Weiss, *Beyond Love* (Colorado Springs: Discovery Press, 2009).
4. For more information on certification or continuing education, visit the American Association for Sex Addition Therapy online at http://www.aasat.org.

About the Author

Dr. Douglas Weiss is a nationally known author, speaker, and licensed psychologist. He is the executive director of Heart to Heart Counseling Center in Colorado Springs. Dr. Weiss oversees a number of counselors, support groups, and three-day intensive workshops. He offers telephone counseling and telephone groups for clients all over the world. Dr. Weiss is the president of the American Association for Sex Addiction Therapy (AASAT). He is a frequent guest in the national television, radio, and print media and a prolific writer on marriage, addiction, and self-help topics. His speaking engagements take him around the world to speak on topics pertaining to intimacy in marriage, singlehood, men's and women's issues, and recovery from addiction. He personally understands sexual addiction, having won his own battle more than twenty years ago. His decades of sobriety give him an edge as a counselor and a unique ability to guide others through the recovery process.

His television appearances include the *Oprah Winfrey Show, Dr. Phil*, ABC's *20/20, 48 Hours, Good Morning America, Winning@Marriage*, and the *Montel Williams Show*, as well as on networks such as CNN, DayStar, Discovery Health, Fox News, and TBN. Dr. Weiss's work and interviews have been published in *Charisma Magazine, Cosmopolitan, Elle, Glamour, Marie Claire, Ministry Today, Redbook, Seven, US News and World Report*, and *USA Today*.

Dr. Weiss is the author of more than twenty books on marriage, men's issues, addiction recovery, and self-help. His titles include *The Final Freedom; Sex, God and Men; Intimacy; The Seven Love Agreements; Get a Grip; The Ten-Minute Marriage Principle; Intimacy Anorexia;* and *The 30-Day Marriage Makeover*. He lives in Colorado Springs with his family.

3 and 5 Day Intensives

TOPICS

- Marriage
- Intimacy Anorexia
- Sexual Addiction
- Sexual Trauma

Spend 3 or 5 days with Dr. Weiss in Colorado Springs, Colorado. Intensives are available every week of the year!

3 Day Intensives

3 Day Intensives offer real solutions for individuals or couples and are designed specifically for you or your marriage. You will leave the Intensive with a plan for success and have opportunities for ongoing support.

5 Day Intensives

5 Day Intensives are designed for those who may have failed in previous treatment, have significant denial, have not fully disclosed or have psychological issues. A 5 Day Intensive gives the individual or couple more time to thoroughly get to their causes and solutions.

www.drdougweiss.com

Sexual Recovery Materials

Intimacy Anorexia Materials

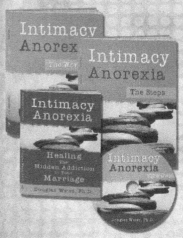

719.278.3708